UNITED ARAB EMIRATES

AN EXPAT'S TRAVEL GUIDE TO MOVING

& LIVING IN THE UAE

PEYTON ROGERS

Copyright ©2018 All rights reserved.

Printed in the United States of America

No part of this book may be reproduced in any written, electronic, recording, or photocopying without written permission of the publisher or author.

ISBN-13: 978-1723156915

ISBN-10: 1723156914

Why I Wrote This Book

For a variety of reasons, there is an increasing number of expats who want to move to a foreign country. Some of the reasons for wanting to relocate include a desire for a more relaxed lifestyle, a higher salary, a better quality of life, a year-round warm climate, and a chance to live in a vibrant, booming metropolitan city. Others are looking for a lower cost of living, a safe place to raise a family, affordable healthcare, a stable government, and cultural exposure. If you are seeking any of these benefits, a logical choice is the United Arab Emirates (UAE). Indeed, the UAE has something for everyone and is recognized as a top travel destination.

Moving can be difficult – even to the UAE, and there is always that family member, friend, book, blog, newsletter, or magazine spreading fear attempting to discourage you from pursuing your dream – moving to a foreign country. Most of the problems that occur during a move come from lack of preparation and poor information. Unfortunately, often there is little information available about the place you want to move to or the information available is not comprehensive enough to be a valuable resource for anyone who wants to embark on this life-changing move. This compounds the difficulties of moving.

What if you had a resource that could easily explain the steps you should take, what you should look out for, what you should expect, where you can get information, and how to avoid the common mistakes and pitfalls that plague most travelers?

This is precisely what *United Arab Emirates: An Expat's Travel Guide to Moving & Living In The UAE* will help you achieve. My desire is to provide you, an expatriate who wants to move and live in the UAE, with an A to Z knowledge about the entire process so that your move is as pleasurable and easy as possible.

Why You Should Read This Book

This book will help you get started on your life-changing journey of moving and living in the UAE. From dining at the finest restaurants in Dubai, visiting the many attractions in Abu Dhabi, hiking in the desert, to learning about some of the challenges you might encounter; this book will give you a truthful account and precise details about the experience of moving and living in the UAE.

United Arab Emirates: An Expat's Travel Guide to Moving and Living In The UAE aims to provide you with the knowledge you will need to get you started on your move to the UAE. From visa information, how to obtain a driver's license, how to get around, determining where to stay, exploring the country's rich culture, the nightlife/entertainment scene, cuisine, and saving money; you will get an in-depth understanding after reading this one simple book.

As you have probably already discovered, there are not many good books available on living and moving to the UAE. The books that are available lack specific detail, are too expensive, or plain boring. Not this one!

This book is fun, informative, easy to read, and full of pertinent information to make your dream of living in the UAE a reality and a pleasant experience.

Table Of Contents

Chapter 1. An Introduction To The UAE
    A BRIEF HISTORY 1
    LOCATION 3
    GEOGRAPHY 4
    DEMOGRAPHICS 5
    LANGUAGES 8
    GOVERNMENT 8
    SAFETY 12
    ECONOMY 14
    EDUCATION 15
    HEALTHCARE 15
    RELIGION 17

Chapter 2. Visa Information
    HOW TO GET A VISA 19
    NEW VISA AND INVESTMENT RULES 27
    SPONSORING FAMILY 27
    SPONSORING PARENTS 29
    A WOMAN SPONSORING HER FAMILY 31
    TRAVELERS BRINGING PETS 31

Chapter 3. Obtaining Housing
    WHERE TO STAY 33
    HOTEL APARTMENTS 34
    APARTMENTS 35

VILLAS 35
　　LOOK OUT FOR HIDDEN RENTAL COSTS 36
　　BUYING VS LEASING 38
Chapter 4. How To Get Around The UAE 41
　　AVAILABLE MODES OF TRANSPORT 41
　　ROAD TRANSPORT 41
　　BUYING VS LEASING 45
　　OUR RENTING VS BUYING EXPERIENCE 49
　　SHIPPING A CAR 51
　　GETTING A DRIVER'S LICENSE 53
　　THE HIDDEN COST OF DRIVING 58
Chapter 5. The Emirati Culture 67
　　THE PEOPLE 67
　　CULTURAL PRACTICES 67
　　CUISINE 68
　　THE DO'S AND DON'TS 69
Chapter 6. Things To Do In The UAE 75
　　UAE ATTRACTIONS 75
　　DUBAI 75
　　ABU DHABI 81
　　AL AIN 84
Chapter 7. Making Money In The UAE 87
　　HOW TO GET A JOB IN THE UAE 87
　　AVAILABLE WORK OPPORTUNITIES 93
　　SALARIES AND WAGES 94

STARTING A BUSINESS	97
FOREIGN INVESTORS	98
Chapter 8. Education In The UAE	**101**
THE SCHOOL SYSTEM	101
PAYING FOR SCHOOL	103
HOMESCHOOL	105
COLLEGES & UNIVERSITIES	105
Chapter 9. Shipping And Mail Service	
MAIL DELIVERY	109
EMIRATES POST	110
METHODS TO BRING ITEMS INTO THE UAE	112
Chapter 10. Leaving The UAE	
CREATE AN EXIT FUND	113
SORTING OUT YOUR WORK CONTRACT	114
SORTING OUT BANK FORMALITIES	115
SORTING OUT YOUR ACCOMMODATION	115
SORTING OUT THINGS WITH SERVICE PROVIDERS	116
SELLING YOUR BELONGINGS	116
SORTING OUT MATTERS WITH PETS	117

About the Author

One Last Thing

CHAPTER 1

AN INTRODUCTION TO THE UAE

When you think of the United Arab Emirates (UAE) what comes to mind? Probably images of Dubai, the tallest building in the world, numerous hotels, expensive cars, super-sized malls, and oil. Well, you are not wrong. But there is more to the UAE than its tall buildings, state of the art infrastructure, desert landscapes, and rich culture and traditions. The UAE is a well-rounded country that can make your life-changing move one of the best decisions you ever made and a memorable experience.

A BRIEF HISTORY

Prior to the formation of the UAE, the seven emirates, or Sheikhdoms, were known as Trucial States, in reference to the treaty relation established with the United Kingdom in 1892, together with Bahrain and Qatar. The treaty established an informal protectorate by Great Britain; the territory was not formally annexed by treaty, grant or lawful means, but the British had ultimate power and jurisdiction. The sheikhs agreed not to dispose of any territory, except to the United Kingdom, and not to enter relationships with any other foreign government other than the United Kingdom without its consent. In return, Great Britain promised to protect the Trucial Coast from all aggression by sea and to help in case of land attack. The British-Trucial Sheikhdoms treaty expired on December 1, 1971.

Bahrain and Qatar became independent prior to the treaty expiring. Bahrain became independent in August and Qatar in September 1971.

The seven emirates became fully independent when the treaty expired. Fearing vulnerability due to loss of British protection, the rulers of Abu Dhabi and Dubai decided to form a union between the two emirates independently, preparing a constitution. They invited the rulers of the other five emirates to join. The two sheikhs agreed that the constitution be written on December 2, 1971. On the same date, at the Dubai Guesthouse Palace, four other emirates agreed to enter the union. With that, the UAE was formed. Both Bahrain and Qatar declined their invitations to join the union. Ras al-Khaimah did not join until 1972.

The Discovery of Oil

The UAE was not always an oil-rich country. In fact, the remarkable increase in revenues accruing in other surrounding countries from oil exports such as Iran, Bahrain, Kuwait, Qatar, and Saudi Arabia remained elusive. The first boreholes drilled in Abu Dhabi by Petroleum Development (Trucial Coast) Ltd (PDTC) were unsuccessful. One notable holed drilled in 1950 at Ras Sadr, a 13,000 foot-deep hole (4,000 meters), taking a year to drill, turned up dry, at the cost of 1 million British Pounds.

It was not until 1958 that oil was first struck by a floating platform rig over Abu Dhabi waters. PDTC had continued its onshore explorations, drilling five more boreholes that were also dry, but on October 27, 1960, the company discovered oil on the coast at the Murban No. 3 well. This proved to be a very successful find producing oil in commercial quantities. In 1962, PDTC became the Abu Dhabi Petroleum Company.

As the oil revenue increased, the country's newfound wealth was almost immediately put to good use. The ruler of Abu Dhabi, Sheik Zayed bin Sultan Al Nahyan, often called the Father of the Nation, began a massive construction program building schools, housing, hospitals, and improving the infrastructure of roads and bridges. When Dubai's oil exports commenced in 1969, the Ruler of Dubai, Sheikh Rashid bin Saeed Al Maktoum, began investing the limited oil reserves found into projects that would lead to revenue diversification – creating the Dubai you see today.

Unfortunately, only a limited amount of oil was discovered in Sharjah and none in the other remaining emirates. This is perhaps why the other emirates are not as well known as its wealthier neighbors – they do not have the revenue source to fund massive construction projects.

LOCATION
The UAE is a relatively small country located in the Middle East along the Arabian Peninsula bordering the Arabian Gulf (called the Persian Gulf in other parts of the world). The country shares a border with Oman to the east and Saudi Arabia to the south along with sharing a

maritime border with Qatar to the west and Iran to the north.

You may wonder why it is important to know where the UAE is located. The reality is that few people bother with the location of any place they visit and even fewer people can find different places on a map, not even their own country! Moving to the UAE will literally mean changing your location, not only by a couple of miles but for possibly thousands of miles away.

It also makes you look good to be able to talk about the country's location to friends and family when telling them about your big move. Prepare yourself for the resounding question that most people will ask, "Where is the UAE located?"

GEOGRAPHY

The UAE is a federation of seven emirates: Abu Dhabi, the largest of the emirates by total land size and population; Dubai; Ajman; Fujairah; Ras al-Khaimah; Sharjah; and Umm al-Quwain. The capital of the UAE is Abu Dhabi. Both Abu Dhabi and Dubai are considered two of the country's cultural and commercial centers, although Dubai is generally more known due to its diverse economy, the Burj Khalifa tower – the tallest building in the world, and cultural diversity.

DEMOGRAPHICS

Based on the latest United Nations estimates in 2018, the current population is approximately 9.5 million people, which ranks the UAE number 93 in the list of countries by population. The UAE has a very diverse population, of which approximately 12% are UAE nationals with the remaining 88% made up of expatriates.

The largest group of non-UAE nationals are South Asians, followed by Asians, and Western expatriates. The UAE National Bureau of Statistics does not publish demographic data in relation to any nationality. In the table below are the top four largest expatriate groups that make up the majority of the population based on estimates provided by each country's embassy.

Nationals from	Population	% of Total Population	Year of Data
India	2,800,000	27.1	2017
Pakistan	1,200,000	12.53	2014
Bangladesh	700,000	11.32	2013
Philippines	679,819	5.49	2014

Indians

As demonstrated in the table above, Indians represent the largest expatriate group living in the UAE and are also the largest population in the country, and are well represented across many areas of employment. Most Indians live in the three largest cities of the UAE – Dubai, Abu Dhabi, and Sharjah. Many Indians are from Kerala and other south Indian states. Indian influence in the

UAE dates back several centuries because of trade and commerce between the Emirates and India. More recently, a large number of Indians have migrated to the UAE to help support the financial, manufacturing, and transport industries. Many Indians have done very well economically having engaged in professional services and entrepreneurship.

Pakistanis

Like Indians, Pakistanis have a long history with the UAE and are the second largest expatriate group. Pakistanis in the UAE dominate the transport sector - from logistics to crane operators, down to taxi drivers. If you frequently ride taxis in Dubai, it will seem like every taxi driver you meet is from Pakistan. Nonetheless, approximately 20% of Pakistanis are white-collar professionals. Although the remaining 80% of Pakistanis are involved in blue-collar work, the overall impact of Pakistanis in the UAE is quite significant. Pakistanis are among the top investors in the UAE market, ranking as the second largest nationality that has purchased property in Dubai.

Bangladeshis

Despite the 2012 freeze on employment visas that restricts Bangladeshi job seekers from joining the workforce, the number of Bangladeshis that remain still represent a sizeable percentage of the population. The ban stemmed from a spike in crimes committed by Bangladeshis. It is expected that the ban on citizens seeking to work in the UAE will be lifted "very soon" as negotiations between UAE ministers and the Bangladesh government continues. Lifting the ban will be good news as Expo 2020 approaches. Many of the 700,000 Bangladeshis in the UAE work in the construction industry and more are needed to complete this very important project.

Filipinos

Dubai is home to the largest population of Filipinos that live abroad, with approximately 450,000 living in the emirate, forming 21.3% of the population, followed by Abu Dhabi, and Al Ain. Filipinos are mostly employed in the services industry, working in customer services roles in retail, telecommunications, medical, education, real estate, and tourism to name a few. You will also see many Filipinos employed as a housemaid or nanny.

Gender Gap

The UAE has the highest gender imbalance in the world with a male/female ratio of 2.75 for the 15-65 age group. This means that there are 275 men for every 100 women, almost three times the population of women in the country.

The gender disparity is not due to any restrictions placed on the number of children a couple can have. The gender gap is largely due to a large number of labor camp workers that come to the UAE to work. This demographic group consists of men, many who are married, that come to the UAE to work for a few years to earn money to send back home.

LANGUAGES

Arabic is the official and national language of the UAE. Emirati people speak a Gulf dialect of Arabic, which differs, slightly from other Arab and Middle Eastern countries.

No need to worry if you do not speak Arabic. English is widely understood and spoken by many Emiratis, especially the educated and younger generation. You will not have a problem communicating in English in any of the seven emirates. Instructions, signs, websites, voice recordings, are provided in English. Many of the expatriate groups that come to the UAE to work also speak English.

Because the UAE has a diverse population with people represented from all over the world, it is common to hear other languages spoken on a regular basis. These will often include Urdu, Hindi, Bengali, Punjab, Nepali, Cebuano, Spanish, and even Russian.

GOVERNMENT

The UAE is a federation of hereditary absolute monarchies. To be more specific, the UAE is a federal monarchy; a federal monarchy is a federation of states (the seven emirates) with a single monarch that serves as head of the federation but retains different monarchs in the various states joined to the federation.

An absolute monarchy is a form of a monarchy in which one ruler has supreme authority and that authority is not restricted by any written laws, legislature, or customs. In contrast, in constitutional monarchies, the head of state's authority is legally bounded or restricted by a constitution or legislature.

Before you pass judgment on the government for not being democratic, understand that the UAE is one of six countries with an absolute monarchy where power is vested in a single person and the monarch is head of the state as well as the government. These countries include Brunei, Oman, Saudi Arabia, Swaziland, and Vatican City. In none of these countries do the people feel oppressed. In the UAE, Emiratis are proud, patriotic, and fiercely loyal to the ruling family. In fact, some will try to convince you that democracies do not work.

Ruling Families

As previously mentioned, the UAE consists of seven emirates and has six ruling houses (Sharjah and Ras al-Khaimah are ruled by the same family).

Abu Dhabi

Abu Dhabi is ruled by the Al Nahyan family. They have been rulers of Abu Dhabi since 1763. When the seven emirates formed to create the UAE, the late Sheikh Zayed bin Sultan Al Nahyan became the first President and Founder of the UAE. He held the post for 33 years. After his death in 2004 at age 86, his son Sheikh Khalifa bin Zayed Al Nahyan became the President of the UAE and ruler of Abu Dhabi. His brother, Sheikh Mohammad bin Zayed Al Nahyan is the Crown Prince (the crown prince is the male heir apparent to the throne in a royal monarchy) of Abu Dhabi and Commander of the Armed Forces.

Dubai

Dubai is ruled by the Al Maktoum family. The Maktoum family has ruled Dubai since 1833. Sheikh Mohammed bin Rashid Al Maktoum is the Ruler of Dubai and Vice President and Prime Minister of the UAE. His son, Sheikh Hamdan bin Mohammed bin Rashid Al Maktoum is the Crown Prince.

Ras al-Khaimah

Ras al-Khaimah has been ruled by the Al Qasimi family since 1819. The current ruler is Sheikh Saud bin Saqer Al Qasimi. He was appointed Crown Prince in 2003 when his father, Sheikh Saqr bin Muhammed Al Qasimi, unexpectedly removed his elder half-brother for openly expressing hostility towards the US-led 2003 invasion of Iraq. This brought him into conflict with the UAE leadership in oil-rich Abu Dhabi that had taken the strategic direction to place the federation of Sheikhdoms under the military protection of the United States. Abu Dhabi, the lead emirate in the UAE, approved of the dismissal and demonstrated support for Sheikh Saud. He assumed leadership on October 27, 2010, after his father's death. His son, Sheikh Mohammed bin Saud al Qasimi is the Crown Prince.

Sharjah

Sharjah has been ruled by the Al Qasimi family since 1820. The current ruler is Sheikh Sultan bin Muhammed Al Qasimi, commonly known as Sheikh Sultan III. He succeeded his brother, Sheikh Khalid bin Mohammed Al Qasimi, as Emir after his assassination on January 25, 1972. He has ruled Sharjah continuously since this time, apart from a six-day period in June 1987, during an attempted coup led by his brother Sheikh Abd al-Aziz bin Muhammed Al Qasimi.

Ajman

Ajman is ruled by the Al Nuaimi family. Sheikh Humaid bin Rashid Al Nuaimi is the Ruler of Ajman.

Umm al-Quwain

Umm al-Quwain is ruled by the Al Mu'alla family. The current ruler, Sheikh Saud bin Rashid Al Mu'alla, assumed leadership on January 2, 2009, after the death of his father Sheikh Rashid III bin Ahmad Al Mu'alla.

Fujarah

Fujarah is ruled by the Al Sharqi family. The current ruler is Sheikh Hamad bin Mohammed Al Sharqi. He became ruler after the death of his father, Sheikh Mohammed bin Hamad Al Sharqi, in 1974. His son, Sheikh Mohammed bin Hamad bin Mohammed Al Sharqi is the Crown Prince of Fujarah.

SAFETY

There is little need to be concerned for your safety in the UAE because it is an extremely safe country. In fact, Numbeo, a website that curates and collates data to develop the world's largest user-contributed database about cities and countries worldwide, ranked Abu Dhabi the safest city in the world. Single women and families with small children boast about feeling safe in public and at home. You will not have to worry about someone snatching your purse, sexual assault, or the senseless mass shootings that occur in the United States. Not that crime does not occur, but it is minimal compared to the crimes that occur in other developed countries with large cities.

The UAE has a very robust and digitalized intelligence and surveillance system. A lot of money was spent on incorporating the best available practices to prevent crime from happening. When you enter the country as a tourist or soon to be resident, your retinas are scanned and your passport is stamped upon arrival. However, information about you is obtained long before you arrive at the airport. For travelers to the UAE that require a visa, a thorough background check is performed. It is very common for people to have their visa application denied, particularly if the traveler's place of origin is from a country that is involved in an internal conflict or has active terrorist extremist groups. Terrorism is something the country has no tolerance for. The UAE does not support countries that harbor terrorist or finance terrorism. The UAE joined Saudi Arabia, Bahrain,

Oman, and Egypt in breaking ties with Qatar because of its relationship with Iran.

The police are often not highly visible and very few openly carry guns. However, just because you do not see them do not assume that they are not there. There is no shortage of police officers and many of them do not wear a uniform or travel in a police car. Trust assured when you are out in public you are being watched. The number of cameras in Dubai and Abu Dhabi rivals that of Washington, DC and London. If a person commits a crime and is sought after by the police, they are usually found within a few days. Needless to say, they will not be able to leave by getting a flight out of the country.

Aside from the many tourists that travel to the UAE each year, one of the reasons the UAE is a safe place to live is because there are a large number of people that come to the UAE to work. As previously mentioned, the majority of people living in the UAE are expatriates that work under an employment visa. For many expats, working in the UAE offers a chance to earn more money than what they could receive in their home country. More often than not, the money they earn is needed to help support family back home. Therefore, they are not coming to the UAE with the expressed intent to commit a crime. Additionally, the background check and the amount of information collected to obtain an employment visa is thorough and comprehensive. If any red flags are uncovered, your employment visa will not be approved and you will not be allowed to come to the UAE to work.

Individuals that commit a crime are jailed without bail. Once they have served their sentence, they are deported back to their home country. They will not be allowed to enter the UAE again.

ECONOMY

The UAE has a robust economy ranking 27 out of 191 countries in the world in gross domestic product and is positioned number two in the Gulf Cooperation Council (GCC) behind Saudi Arabia. Since achieving independence in 1971, the UAE's economy has grown by nearly 231 times. Economic growth and the free flow of funds has helped the country draw attention as one of the best nations in the world for doing business. In the 2018 *Doing Business Report* published by the World Bank, the UAE ranked 21st, up five spots from 26th in 2017.

The UAE has worked hard to diversify its economy and now has the most diversified economy in the GCC. However, the UAE remains extremely reliant on oil. Abu Dhabi still has vast oil reserves and has remained relatively conservative in its approach to diversification. As such, Abu Dhabi still relies heavily upon oil to fund its economy. Dubai, which has much smaller oil reserves, has been much bolder in diversification. Dubai has grown aggressively and has spent billions to enhance its infrastructure, railway system, while developers have built amazing hotels and commercial and residential property. This growth and diversification strategy has led to Dubai becoming the top tourism destination in the Middle East, and the fifth most popular tourism destination in the world. People from all over the world come to see the Burj Khalifa, the tallest building in the world.

Dubai's incredible growth and risk taking have not always been positive. Dubai suffered from the 2007-2010 financial crisis and had to be bailed out by Abu Dhabi's oil. Dubai has since recovered from the 2007 crisis and is now running on a balanced budget.

EDUCATION

Prior the country's President and Founder of the UAE, the late Sheikh Zayed Bin Sultan Al Nahyan (may God have mercy upon him), the federation of seven emirates did not always equally value education. This attitude changed under Sheikh Zayed's leadership and he made a focus on improving education a countrywide initiative. He once said, "The greatest use that can be made of wealth is to invest it in creating generations of educated and trained people." At present, the UAE has a literacy rate of 95%. Still, more work is underway to lift educational standards. Many initiatives are being implemented across all levels, ensuring that students are prepared to compete in the global marketplace.

HEALTHCARE

Access to a good doctor, dentist, hospital, and healthcare facilities is not a problem in the UAE. There are government run hospitals, privately run clinics, and doctors represented from every developed country in the world practicing medicine in the UAE. Indeed, the country has benefited from medical tourists from all over the GCC. The UAE attracts medical tourists seeking cosmetic surgery and other beautification treatment, and advanced procedures including cardiac spinal surgery, cancer treatment, and dental treatment, as health services are performed at a higher standard than other Arab countries in the region. That does not mean that you may not prefer to have specific types of treatments done abroad.

Overall, health care in the UAE is well managed by the Ministry of Health, which monitors the public health sector for the northern emirates. Abu Dhabi and Dubai are overseen by separate health authorities. In February 2008, the Ministry of Health unveiled a five-year health strategy that focuses on unifying health care policy and improving access to healthcare services at a reasonable cost, at the same time reducing dependence on overseas treatment.

Abu Dhabi introduced mandatory health insurance for all expatriates and their dependents. Abu Dhabi nationals were brought under the scheme in June 2008 and Dubai followed suit by offering health insurance to all government employees. Eventually, under federal law, every Emirati and every expatriate permanent resident living in the country will be covered by compulsory health insurance under a unified mandatory scheme.

In general, the UAE maintains a high position in the healthcare index produced by the World Health Organization, which measures overall health system performance across the world. In 2018, the UAE ranked

27 out of 191 countries, beating Australia, Canada, United States of America, and even Costa Rica.

RELIGION

The predominant religion observed in the UAE is Islam. Islam is the official state religion of the UAE. If you are not Muslim, there is no need to worry. The government follows a policy of tolerance toward other religions and very rarely interferes in the activities of non-Muslims. However, you are strictly prohibited from openly proselytizing on the street or through any form of media. Do not try to impose your religious views on others, especially Muslims, while you are in the UAE and you will not have any trouble.

Non-Muslims are allowed to have church services in designated areas within the city, which is usually a compound made up of small protestant and catholic churches. You are allowed to have small gatherings in your home if you like. However, if the group gets to large you may attract unwanted attention.

CHAPTER 2

VISA INFORMATION

So you want to come to the UAE? No matter the reason you are planning to travel to the UAE – whether tourism, business or work, even to study, you will need to obtain a visa.

HOW TO GET A VISA

There are two general types of visas – short-term and long-term. The short-term visa allows you to stay in the UAE for no more than 90 days. The long-term visa is your residency stamp, which allows you to stay indefinitely provided certain conditions are met. Your nationality will determine whether you are allowed to obtain an entry permit or visa with or without a sponsor.

Nationals of countries requiring a prearranged UAE visa can apply and pay for visas online. The UAE provides many channels for online visas. Nationals from a select group of countries can get a visa on arrival.

Visit Visa

The visit visa or entry permit into the UAE requires sponsorship from a citizen, resident, or investor. This visa is for nationals that are not eligible for a *Visa On Arrival.*

UAE Nationals and residents can apply online and acquire 30-day/90-day UAE visit visa or entry permit for their families, friends, and relatives through the Ministry of Interior website and the UAE-MOI app on smartphones. The processing period may take a few days. After the visa is issued, sponsors should send a copy of the permit to their family, friends, relatives (recipient) by fax or email. It is necessary for recipients to possess a copy of the entry permit before leaving their country of origin. The sponsor should submit the original permit to the airport.

Tourist Visa

A Tourist visa is a special visa category under visit visa, which can be obtained for eligible tourists around the world. The visa permits the holder to stay for a duration of 30 days. The visa requires sponsorship of UAE airlines, hotels and tour operators who bring in visitors.

A UAE-based airline can arrange a visa on your behalf – they can process it through the official visa issuing authorities. Each airline has some general or specific conditions, which must be met in order for your visa to be arranged by them. One of them is you must fly with them instead of another airline.

Licensed travel agents and hotels in the UAE can arrange a tourist visa for you provided you purchase the ticket through them and maintain a hotel reservation with them. It is important to check the authenticity of travel agents to ensure they are a legitimate business and not a fraud. You should refrain from paying or sending copies of your official documents until you are certain the travel agent is trustworthy.

Visa On Arrival

If you are a passport holder of one of the countries or territories listed below, no advance arrangements are required to visit the UAE. Simply disembark your flight at the airport and proceed to immigration, where your passport will be stamped with a 30-day visit visa free of charge.

Andorra, Australia, Brunei, Canada, China, Hong Kong, Ireland, Japan, Malaysia, Mauritius, Monaco, New Zealand, Russia, San Marino, Singapore, Ukraine, United Kingdom, United States of America, Vatican City

If you are a passport holder from of one of the countries or territories listed below, your passport will be stamped with a multiple entry 90-day visit visa that is valid for 6 months from the date of issue, and for a stay of 90 days total.

Argentina, Austria, Belgium, Bulgaria, Chile, Croatia, Cyprus, Czech Republic, Denmark, Estonia, Finland, France, Germany, Greece, Hungary, Iceland, Italy, Latvia, Liechstein, Lithuania, Luxemburg, Malta, Netherlands, Norway, Poland, Portugal, Romania, Seychelles, Slovakia, Slovenia, South Korea, Spain, Sweden, Switzerland

Citizens of the European countries listed above are also entitled to apply for a pre-arranged visit visa if the 'on arrival 90 day visa' has been fully utilized, or if they wish to use the pre-arranged visa.

Residency

There are two ways to obtain residency: sponsorship by an employer or by investing in property.

Residency by Employment

Before you can work in the UAE, you must have a residency visa. Your employer must apply for the residency visa on your behalf by receiving approval from the Ministry of Labor. The company's personnel relations officer (PRO) normally completes the process for you. A permanent residency visa is typically valid for 3 years. The process is as follows:

Step 1. First, the employer will obtain approval from the Ministry of Labor. The basic purpose of this is that the Ministry of Labor wants to make sure that there are no unemployed local citizens in the country who can perform the job.

Step 2. The Ministry of Labor issues an Entry Permit Visa, which is also called a 'Pink Visa' because it is printed on pink paper. The Entry Permit allows the applicant to enter the UAE. After arrival, the sponsoring company will have 60 days to complete the process of obtaining the residence visa. The permit is valid for two months from the date of issue. The applicant is allowed to work during this period.

Special Note: If you have already entered the UAE on a visit visa, it is possible to transfer to a residence visa by either re-entering the UAE with your sponsor entry permit or by filing for a change of status application at one of the typing centers or by visiting the local Immigration Department.

Step 3. You will then go to the Emirates ID service for the ID. You should take your passport and entry permit (which was issued by the Ministry of Labor) with you.

Special Note: The Emirates ID is your official identify card and serves as your labor card. The card displays your picture, full name, nationality, date of birth, gender, and your signature. The expiry date is the official day your residency ends, if not renewed.

Step 4. The employer will apply to the immigration authorities for your Permanent Resident Visa. Meanwhile, you will need to go to a government hospital for the Medical Fitness Test to show that you are 'Fit to Work.'

Step 5. Once the employer has your Medical Fitness Test, they will go to the Department of Naturalization and Residency with all your documents. There, your passport will be stamped with a work visa.

This completes the process. You are now a legal resident.

Investor Visa

Property investors can hold residency without employer sponsorship. Investors can either apply for a residency permit (Property Investor Visa) – renewable every two years and applicable to Dubai properties only, or a residence visa (Six Months Residency Visa) – renewable every six months for homes purchased in another emirate. The principal difference between the residency permit and the residency visa is that the residence permit for property owners is renewable every two years (for properties purchased in Dubai), whereas the residence visa property allows multiple-entry for property owners and is renewable every six months. With the residency permit, you become a UAE resident meaning you can obtain an Emirates ID, UAE driving license, and sponsor family as well. To be eligible for either the residence permit or visa, properties must be valued at more than 1 million Dhs. You are allowed to mortgage the property for the residence permit, but if the property is mortgaged a minimum 50% of the original purchase price must be paid off. In other words, if the property's value is 2 million Dhs, 1 million Dhs must be paid off.

Verification of the investment requirement is undertaken by the Dubai Land Development for the residence permit and the relevant immigration authority for the residence visa. There is a minimum monthly income requirement of 10,000 Dhs or equivalent in foreign currency. The investor's income source may come from inside our outside the UAE.

Investment Criteria

The investment property must be valued at more than 1 million Dhs. If more than one investor owns the property, the shared value must be more than1 million Dhs. The property must be in a freehold area and entirely owned by the investor, with the title deed issued in the name of the applicant. If the investors are married, a legal marriage certificate will have to be provided. Lease-to-own deeds are not accepted. Commercial properties are not allowed. Only residential properties are permitted for the purposes of the visas. In addition to this, the property must be "habitable" – in other words, it must be in good condition and suitable for someone to live in.

Documentation Required

The standard documentation required to obtain either a residence permit or visa includes copies of passports and current visas, passport photo, police clearance certificates, title deeds, marriage certificates, attested bank statements, proof of health insurance for applicants and dependents, and a utility bill.

How Much Does It Cost

The residence permit costs approximately 13,000 Dhs to 15,000 Dhs in government fees, with the higher end inclusive of the police clearing letter (220 Dhs), administration fee (420 Dhs), application costs (3,000 Dhs), typing and entry permit (1,000 Dhs), DED license insurance (8,440 Dhs) and stamping/Emirates ID/Medical (2,490 Dhs). If the investor is sponsoring dependents, there is an additional (5,000 Dhs to 6,000 Dhs) deposit for each dependent, inclusive of Emirates ID/Medical. Estimated government fees for the residence visa are considerably less at 2,300 Dhs per applicant, which is the same for each dependent. However, this visa must be renewed every six months (1,100 Dhs each time) so the costs can add up. Fees apply for sponsorship of family and renewal (250 Dhs).

Things to Watch Out For

Important factors to bear in mind include the following:

- Spouse and dependents are subject to fulfilling the dependent's sponsorship criteria.
- Sponsorship of domestic workers (a nanny or maid) is allowed under the residence permit. However, under the residence visa, sponsorship of domestic workers is subject to approval from the relevant immigration authority.
- An in-country medical examination is required for investors applying for a residence permit.
- Neither the resident permit nor the residence visa status leads to citizenship.
- Holders of the residence permit or the residence visa are prohibited from working.
- There is no maximum period of stay for both the residence permit and the residence visa. However,

holders of the residence permit should not stay outside of the UAE for more than six consecutive months or risk having your permit canceled.
- The Department of Economic Development issues an investor's license for every permit granted. The license is valid for four years and renewable thereafter.

NEW VISA AND INVESTMENT RULES

On May 22, 2018, via a Cabinet resolution, it was announced the UAE would begin offering residency visas valid for up to 10 years for investors and specialists such as doctors and engineers. The system is meant to increase the number of specialists in medical, scientific research and technical fields, as well as all scientists and innovators, including entrepreneurs by offering a longer-term visa incentive. The families of these expatriates will also receive the same visa duration. Top performing students are also eligible for the 10-year residency visa.

SPONSORING FAMILY

Expatriate residents - employers and employees, may sponsor their families in the UAE provided they have a valid residency visa and certain conditions are met. Male residents who are employed in the UAE can sponsor their immediate family members, such as their wife and children, subject to conditions, which include a minimum monthly salary of 4,000 Dirhams (Dhs) or 3,000 Dhs plus accommodation. To sponsor his wife, the expatriate resident must prove an existing marital relationship by submitting an authenticated marriage certificate in

Arabic or translated into Arabic by a certified translator. An expatriate resident can sponsor his daughter(s) only if she/they are unmarried. The expatriate resident can sponsor his son(s) only up to the age of 18. If after the age of 18, the son is studying in the UAE or abroad, he can be sponsored until the age of 21, by providing proof that he is studying. However, in order for his residence visa to remain valid, he has to enter the UAE at least once every six months. The resident will need to place a deposit with the respective General Directorate of Residency and Foreign Affairs (GDRFA) for his son's visa.

An expatriate resident can sponsor their stepchildren, subject to GDRFA conditions, which include a deposit for each child and a written no-objection letter from the biological parent. Their residence visas are valid for one year - renewable annually.

Sponsored residents, except adult males who are continuing their education and sponsored parents, can enjoy the same visa duration as their sponsors. For adult males and parents, the residence visa is granted on a yearly basis regardless of the sponsor's visa duration. The conditions are subject to change from time to time. You should check with the GDRFA of the respective emirate.

A resident sponsor has 30 days to apply for his dependent's residence visa after they enter the UAE and to modify their status from an entry permit to a resident visa holder. Family members will be issued a visa for one, two, or three years depending on the nature of the work and labor contract of the sponsoring member and his capacity as an employee or employer.

Required Documents to Sponsor Wife and Children

- Online application or through a registered typing office
- Passport copies of wife and children
- Passport size photos of wife and children
- Medical clearance certificate for the wife and children above 18 years old
- Copy of the husband's employment contract or company contract
- Salary certificate from the employer stating the employee's monthly wage
- Marriage certificate
- Registered tenancy contract
- Latest utility bill

SPONSORING PARENTS

An expatriate employee can sponsor his parents for a year's stay by paying a deposit as a guarantee for each parent as stipulated by the respective immigration department. An expatriate cannot sponsor only one of his parents. He needs to sponsor both parents together. He also needs to provide proof that he is their sole support and that they have no one else who could take care of them back home. If one of the parents has passed away or if the parents are divorced, he has to show the related official documents as justification to sponsor only one of the parents. In addition to providing the aforementioned supporting documentation, the expatriate sponsor must earn the minimum salary stipulated and obtain a medical insurance policy for parents with the minimum coverage stipulated for each, to be renewed each year.

According to the Dubai Government, the General Directorate of Residency Affairs – Dubai (DNRD) stipulates a minimum salary of 20,000 Dhs or a monthly pay of 19,000 Dhs plus a two-bedroom accommodation to sponsor a parent.

My Personal Experience Sponsoring a Parent

If you need to sponsor a parent, I strongly suggest that you live in Dubai. I tried to sponsor my father-in-law in Abu Dhabi and was unsuccessful. We submitted all the necessary paper work required to the GDRFA: an authenticated marriage certificate showing I am legally married to his daughter; birth certificate showing he is my wife's father; death certificate of his spouse to prove that he is the only living parent; a medical statement providing proof that he is visually impaired; my salary certificate, three months of bank statements, current lease agreement, copies of my passport, visa page, and Emirates ID. Despite being able to check all the necessary boxes, my application to sponsor my father-in-law was denied. No explanation was given. This outcome may be to the fact that we do not have 'wasta' backing us. Wasta is an Arabic word that translates as something like authority, influence, political power, connections, or a combination of those terms. The common English expression "It's not what you know but who you know" is a good equivalent for wasta.

A WOMAN SPONSORING HER FAMILY
In Abu Dhabi, a woman can sponsor her husband and children if she holds a residence permit stating that she is an engineer, teacher, doctor, nurse or any other profession related to the medical sector, and if her monthly salary is not less than 10,000 Dhs or 8,000 Dhs plus accommodation.

In Dubai, if a woman is not employed in one of the above-mentioned categories she may still get approval to sponsor her family if her monthly salary is more than 10,000 Dhs and with special permission from the DNRD.

A single mother can sponsor her child. The authorities may ask for documents similar to those required to sponsor stepchildren.

TRAVELERS BRINGING PETS
To bring a pet into the UAE will require you to obtain an Import Permit from the Ministry of Environment and Water. The easiest way is to create a user account on the organization's website and follow the instructions. Through the e-service, you will be able to submit all the required documents by email and obtain detailed information on necessary documents and regulations. To obtain the permit, you will need a vaccination card or veterinarian health certificate for each dog or cat, and your passport copy and a microchip number clearly displayed on the vaccine book or microchip certificate.

Some pets will need a rabies test in advance of entry 12 weeks before entering the UAE. All pets entering the UAE must travel as manifest cargo.

Below is a list of dog breeds the UAE has been banned from entry.

1. Pit Bull Terrier (American or any other hybrid)
2. Rottweilers (or any other hybrid)
3. Japanese Tosa (Tosa Inu; Tosa Fighting Dog)
4. Argentinian Fighting Dog (Dogo Argentino; Argentinian Mastiff)
5. Brazilian Fighting Dog (Fila Brasileino; Brazilian Mastiff)
6. Wolf Dog Hybrid (Any dog mixed with a wolf)
7. Staffordshire Terrier (American or any other hybrid)
8. Boxers
9. Mastiffs (or any Mastiff Hybrid)
10. Doberman
11. Canano Presa
12. Cross breeds with an extract of the above listed breeds

CHAPTER 3

OBTAINING HOUSING

Once you have secured a job and have relocated to the UAE your most important decision will be where you will stay. Your options will be determined by the size of your budget. Luckily, there is suitable accommodation available for every budget.

WHERE TO STAY

Having a roof over your head in a foreign land is something you need to give considerable thought. You will not have long before the free nights at the hotel provided by the company that brought you over will run out. Therefore, you need to act quickly but be deliberate in doing plenty of research to avoid making a hasty decision that you may later regret. Lease contracts are generally for one year and the rent is paid upfront in one installment; however, the upfront payment requirement is starting to change in some areas.

If you will be searching for your own accommodation and you have a family, you will need to consider the size of the property and the location relative to schools and your job. Location is always important, as this will dictate how much you will pay. Rental prices in Abu Dhabi are often higher than Dubai. Prices in the northern emirates such as Sharjah, Ajman, and Ras Al Khaimah are much cheaper than Dubai. However, there is another price to pay. Commuting from Sharjah and Ajman to Dubai is extremely slow with stop-and-go traffic and people mashing their brakes. What you save in money will cost you in commuting time. To begin your search, a great website to start is at Propertyfinder.ae.

If you are single and unsure about what part of the city you want to live, you may consider renting a room in an already tenanted apartment or villa. However, bear in mind that the government frowns upon unmarried males and females sharing accommodation. Whereas this practice may be perfectly acceptable in your home country, this is the UAE and things have not progressed to this level yet. Officially, it is not sanctioned in any emirate, although Dubai is much more liberal and unlikely to impose a penalty on non-Muslims for sharing a house. The other emirates are not as forgiving.

HOTEL APARTMENTS

Hotel apartments are a good option in the short-term if you are unsure of where you want to stay. It will cost you more than renting an apartment, but it allows you to live there indefinitely without signing a lease. Hotel apartments come with the flexibility of monthly or annual payments. They also offer many amenities. The one-bedroom units are often very spacious, fully furnished with excellent housekeeping services, include high-speed internet, a business center, fitness center, and utilities are included in the price. Some even offer valet parking – all at prices similar to some luxury one-bedroom flats. It is like living in a cozy home but with all the luxuries and services you get in a hotel. Hotel apartments mostly cater to long-term business tourists, single men and women, or working couples. Unfortunately, there are not many two or three bedroom hotel apartments for families.

APARTMENTS

If you plan to rent an apartment, you will have to find out how much of the rent is required up front. In the past, it was necessary to pay the whole 12 months up front. If you did not have the money, landlords required you to pay an initial deposit of three months and provide postdated checks for the outstanding amount. Most people do not have three months of rent in cash, so they had to get a loan for this amount from a bank. Things have eased a bit and it may be possible to get an agent to negotiate a better deal for you. An agent may help to lower your lease, but their services are not free.

VILLAS

If you have a large family or expect to have lots of houseguests, then you may want to consider leasing a villa. A villa will provide you with more bedrooms, bathrooms, livable space, and some have an outside garden area. Many villas have a maid accommodation that can often be used as a nursery. Many villas come with pools. Similar to apartments, you will have to sign a one-year lease and be prepared to pay the annual lease upfront in one payment before occupying the property.

The thing to think about when looking at villas is the age of the villa and how committed are the landlord and Management Company to doing essential maintenance.

Try to speak with tenants living in the other villas about this.

Because of their larger size, villas are more difficult to cool. While you may not need to use the air conditioner much, if at all, during the winter, it will be essential over the summer. Look for villas that have an individual air conditioner in each room as opposed to those that have central air. This will help to reduce the utility bill.

The price of villas has come down a lot in Abu Dhabi and Dubai. You can get some good deals if you live further away from the city center. There is a lot more competition these days and landlords have had to be more flexible on pricing. I have seen the price go down by 15,000 Dhs in one year in the villa compound I live in. In some villa compounds, the price dropped by 30,000 Dhs. Right now, there is more supply than demand. You can negotiate the price directly with the landlord or management company or enlist the help of an agent.

LOOK OUT FOR HIDDEN RENTAL COSTS
Aside from the actual rent, there are additional costs that can shock you if you are not aware of them. Keep in mind the following costs when renting in Dubai.

Agency Fees

By law in the UAE, agents are entitled to receive a fee when a tenancy contract is signed. Usually, their commission is 5% of the annual rent. There is no clause stating that agents hold the right to continue receiving that fee every time a contract is renewed. In fact, agents have no right to claim an additional fee if the contract is renewed between the tenant and the landlord, as the procedure does not require and kind of facilitation from the part of the agent. However, some agents do slip a renewal fee in the contract and if the tenant unintentionally agreed by signing that contract, he or she is compelled to honor whatever is stated in the contract and is, therefore, obliged to pay a fee upon renewal.

Agents do not have access to a Multiple Listing Service (MLS) like real estate brokers use in the United States to share information about properties. They only work with a select group of landlords and management companies and cannot show you another company's properties. Really, you do not have to use an agent if you do not want to. If you see a property you like, you can contact the management company or landlord directly to have them show you the unit.

Favorably, because of pricing pressure on rents right now, attracting tenants has become very competitive. Therefore, many companies are not charging the customer an agency fee. This fee is most likely being passed to the Landlord.

Ejari Fee

Ejari system is a legal contract registration platform by Dubai's Land Department helping to authenticate rental contracts and agreement between tenants and landlords. The standard fee is 195 Dhs, valid for all types of properties.

Housing Fee

A Dubai municipal fee of 5% is assessed on annual rent paid in 12 equal parts (along with every rental payment) and added to the Dubai Electricity and Water Authority (DEWA) bills.

DEWA

You will have to pay a DEWA deposit when renting a property. The deposit amount is as follows:

- Apartment: 2,000 Dhs (deposit - refund on leaving), 110 Dhs (connection, non-refundable)
- Villa: 4,000 Dhs (deposit – refund on leaving);110 Dhs (connection, non-refundable)

District Cooling Fees

District cooling deposits and connection fees vary according to the provider and the size of the property.

Security Deposit

Some landlords will require a security deposit equivalent to one month's rent. The deposit is fully refundable when your lease expires and when you vacate the property. Some landlords will deduct a certain amount from the deposit for the repainting of walls and minor repairs.

BUYING VS LEASING

Buying is an option you may want to consider. Unlike many countries where foreign investment is discouraged, in Abu Dhabi and Dubai, it is possible to buy property in select developments. Many expats do opt to buy rather than rent. If your company provides a housing allowance paid directly to you in cash, this can be used to cover your mortgage. This is what the smart money does; they have their employer indirectly pay for their investment property. Otherwise, you end up giving away money that can be used to acquire ownership for yourself to someone else.

CHAPTER 4

HOW TO GET AROUND THE UAE

After you have successfully secured affordable accommodation, another important thing you need to plan for is how to get around the UAE. No need to worry. Traveling in the UAE is not difficult. The country has a good road network and public transportation system, taxis, a rail system if you live in Dubai, and access to private drivers.

AVAILABLE MODES OF TRANSPORT

There are several modes of transportation available in the UAE so it is really for you to choose the one that will be best for you. You can choose to use land transportation by either car, bus, motorcycle, or taxi.

ROAD TRANSPORT
Bus

Traveling within Emirates

Many chose to travel by bus, as this is the least expensive option. Public bus transportation is available in Abu Dhabi and Dubai. Since its launch in 2008, the Department of Transport (DOT) in Abu Dhabi has enhanced the coverage and quality of its bus services at all levels. The Bus Office now operates over 650 buses on over 95 service routes within different regions of the emirate of Abu Dhabi. You can visit the Department of Transport website to view the regional bus schedule. The

Dubai Road & Transport Authority (RTA) is responsible for bus service in Dubai.

Traveling Between Emirates

You do not need a car to travel from Abu Dhabi to Dubai and vice versa. While in the past this may have been true, both the DOT and RTA have worked together to provide a sensible, low-cost way of traveling between the emirates. The cost is 25 Dhs one-way. This is by far the cheapest way to get from Abu Dhabi to Dubai without having your own car. The travel time takes between one and a half to two hours.

Motorcycle

Travel by motorcycle is the next cheapest form of transportation. The cost of ownership is generally much lower than a car. People with a driving license from one of 41 listed countries can directly transfer their license by going into any DOT or RTA Office with the necessary documentation and fee. If you do not already have a motorcycle license, you will have to take a motorcycle course. The minimum age requirement for a motorcycle driving license course is 17 years old.

Although motorcycles have been growing in popularity, especially in Dubai, riders should exercise extreme caution. Drivers do not look out for you. Other than the restaurant delivery drivers on motorbikes, there simply are not that many bikers on the road. Therefore, it is necessary for motorcycle riders to be defensive drivers. The weather also makes riding a motorcycle difficult.

Although road conditions are extremely good, it is too hot to wear proper leathers. Cotton mesh is a good substitute for leather, but this is also too hot for the UAE.

Personally, I do not recommend anyone become a motorcyclist in the UAE. Riding for recreational purposes, once or twice during the week or on weekends, is safer. But, if you absolutely have to ride more than this, just remember to be a defensive driver.

Car

Travel by car is the most popular and preferred way of getting around the country. If you will not be shipping a car to the UAE, there are plenty of cars available for you to purchase or lease when you arrive. All the major car manufacturers have a showroom here so finding a new or pre-owned car will not be difficult. No matter how large or small your car budget may be, trust that there is something for you.

The price of gas (petrol for some) is also reasonable compared to prices in Europe and other parts of the world. Expect to see gas prices similar to what you would observe in the United States. At the time of this writing, the per-liter price for gas is as follows:

	AED (Dhs)	Dollars $	British Pounds £	Euros €
Super 98	2.56	0.70	0.53	0.60
Special 95	2.45	0.67	0.50	0.57
E-Plus 9	2.37	0.65	0.49	0.55

| Diesel | 2.66 | 0.72 | 0.55 | 0.62 |

For Americans used to seeing gas priced by the gallon, this equates to $2.65 for Super, $2.54 for Special, $2.46 for Plus, and $2.73 for Diesel.

Taxi

Getting a taxi in the UAE is very easy. There are literally thousands of taxis in Abu and Dubai waiting to drive you to your destination. Just stand along the street and motion with your hand to hail a taxi. Whether or not the taxi driver knows how to get to your destination is a different story. Taxis do not have a GPS system. Very rarely will the taxi driver have cellular data that enables them to use Google Maps or Waze on their mobile phone. It is better to have some idea of where you want to go and how to get there.

Taxis are not super expensive but they are also not cheap. You will not want to use them as your primary means of transportation each day, particularly if you have to travel long distances. The only advantage is they are available 24 hours a day and will drive you as far as you want to go. Be prepared to pay in cash. In Dubai, not all taxis are equipped to accept payment via a credit or debit card. There are no taxis able to accept payment with a card in Abu Dhabi.

Uber

Uber is only available in Dubai and works the same as in other cities around the world. However, Uber is not widely used because in many cases taxis are cheaper and more readily available. With Uber, you have to request a driver and wait for them to arrive.

BUYING VS LEASING

If you make the choice to drive, one of the biggest decisions you will need to make is whether to buy or lease a vehicle. There are compelling reasons to consider both. The question is which is best for you while you are in the UAE.

If you plan to stay in the UAE for more than four years and can afford to pay for a vehicle outright, or can make the required monthly payment, the best choice may be to purchase a new vehicle. Buying a new car is generally worth it if you are going to keep the car for the long term – more than four years. After paying off the car, you are free to do whatever you want with it. You can continue to drive it, sell it, give it away, etc. The good thing is after it is paid off you no longer have to worry about monthly payments. Of course, there is always the ongoing maintenance that is required. You will also be responsible for registering your vehicle each year and passing the vehicle inspection.

Unless your car is less than three years old, vehicle inspections are compulsory when you renew your car registration, buy a second-hand car, import a car, change vehicle's chassis or engine, or are requested by the police to change your vehicle's tires. The car will have to undergo a comprehensive vehicle inspection at one of the many designated vehicle inspection centers (VIC).

Provided is a summary of what you should expect at the VIC:

1. Visit any VIC during working hours. It is best that you check to see if you have any fines linked to the car that you are planning to register and pay them in advance.
2. Drive your car through the test lane.
   Note: Testing is required if your car is older than three years. Go directly to the registration office and take a ticket to cue if your vehicle is less than three years old.
3. Obtain your vehicle test certificate.
   - If your vehicle passes, you are given a vehicle test certificate.
   - If it fails, you must repair any required parts and revisit the test lane before your current registration expires.
   - Buy your car insurance and obtain the vehicle insurance certificate. Upon receiving the vehicle test certificate and car insurance, take a ticket and wait until your turn comes to receive your vehicle registration card.
4. Obtain a vehicle registration card from the Police Officer or a service machine, whichever is available.
5. Once the above-mentioned process has been completed, you will then be able to receive a license

plate (for a first-time owner) and a sticker that shows the month and year the car was registered.

Make sure you have the following items with you when you visit the VIC:

- Your old car registration card
- Your Emirates ID
- Your valid UAE driving license
- The vehicle insurance certificate
- The vehicle test certificate

If you purchase a new car, you can ask the car dealer to complete the vehicle registration and car insurance process for you. You will have to pay the required fees, but you can avoid the lines at the VIC.

A long-term car lease (usually for one year or more) allows you to avoid the hassles of ownership – pesky details like maintenance, vehicle registration, and car insurance. These items are included in the lease price. Both car rental companies and car dealers offer lease options. The car rental companies offer more short-term lease options whereas car dealers require a minimum lease period of one year. The rule of thumb is the longer the lease period, the lower the lease price with the maximum period of 48 months, or four years. Another benefit of leasing is when the lease expires, leasers have the option to buy the car at a predefined value, extend the period for the same car at a lower rate, start a lease on another vehicle, or turn the car in and walk away. That is the key difference between buying versus leasing. With leasing, you avoid the hassle of maintenance and other issues, but by buying you end up owning an asset, albeit a depreciating one.

Many individuals start with a short-term lease on a standard four-door sedan like a Mitsubishi Lancer or a Toyota Corolla that rents for about 1,800 Dhs per month. After a while, most people will generally desire a larger, safer vehicle, especially after observing a large number of massive SUVs barreling down the street. While purchasing a new vehicle may end up costing more, a small bank loan spread over three years for a Ford Explorer a couple of years old could cost around 1,500 Dhs per month. You can get substantially more vehicle for less per month.

Be careful when purchasing used cars. There are plenty of stories of unlucky people that purchased second hand cars from car dealers and private sellers. Used car dealers are the same in every country. They will tell you anything to sell you a car. Beyond that, they also have access to technology that can roll back the mileage on vehicles. Others will tell you to trust them because they can show you a Carfax report. These reports are not full proof and can sometimes be fake.

Purchasing a car from a private seller comes with its own set of risk. When repairs are needed, many buyers later discover that the previous owner made repairs using non-genuine parts, so in order to fix the vehicle properly they must purchase genuine agency parts that are more costly.

I know a man that purchased a used Mercedes from an acquaintance. The car looked good and ran fine. However, the vehicle did not pass inspection. When he took the car to the VIC, he was asked whether the car had been in an accident because the chassis was bent. The man had to sell the car for junk because the cost of repair was more than the car was worth.

Buying a second hand car in the UAE can be a bit of a gamble. However, if you can find a car in good condition at a reasonable price it makes sense. If you plan to own the car for more than two years, buying a car is generally cheaper than leasing.

OUR RENTING VS BUYING EXPERIENCE

Like many people, my wife and I started out by renting cars. She rented cars the size of a Nissan Altima and I rented cars the size of a Toyota Yaris. We learned rather quickly that is it cheaper to pay for a monthly rental instead of paying daily and weekly rental rates. If you opt for a two-week rental, thinking that you will have your car situation sorted by then, and end up needing another week, you will pay more than if you had gotten the monthly rental. We paid approximately 2,100 Dhs and 1,800 Dhs for our rentals, respectively. This was much more than the 3,000 Dhs we had budgeted for car transportation each month (excluding gas).

We live in Abu Dhabi and, at the time, my wife worked in Dubai. After seeing how crazy some people drive, she wanted a larger, safer car for the journey to Dubai each day. However, the cost of renting an SUV was slightly over 3,000 Dhs per month. After shopping around, she was able to find a three-year old BMW 730 Li that came with a warranty for 140,000 Dhs. A four-year car loan made the monthly payment slightly more than the price of renting a Toyota 4Runner (approximately 3,200 Dhs). This was a no brainer for her so she purchased the vehicle. The payment was obviously more than we had budgeted, but we had a nice reliable car that got respect on the road. Nevertheless, because the budget was blown I had to find another option to lower our monthly car expense.

I did not want to continue leasing Corollas but I was not interested in making car payments. We already had one car payment and I did not want to take on additional debt. I started looking for used cars I could afford without getting a loan. One of the employees I manage suggested that I look for cars at Emirates Auto Auction in Dubai. The auction provides hundreds of cars each day listed for sale by banks, private sellers, local governments, and auto dealers at bargain prices. As with all auctions, the cars are sold 'As-is' without a warranty. I bid and successfully purchased a fully loaded 2004 Jaguar XJ6 for 7,800 Dhs total. The car had only one owner, good interior and exterior, and had very low miles, but the suspension system and the fuel pump needed replacing. I was able to find used parts in Sharjah that helped to lower the repair cost. In total, after repairs, tinting the windows and installing a backup camera, car insurance and registration, the Jaguar cost me about 21,000 Dhs, which breaks down to about 1,750 Dhs monthly; still lower than the 1,800 Dhs I was spending each month leasing Corollas. Purchasing a car at the auction was a big gamble, but it was worth it. I do not have a car payment or a monthly lease. When we are ready to leave the UAE, I plan to give the car away.

SHIPPING A CAR

If you already own a car that is less than 10 years old, you can have it shipped to the UAE. To ship your car into the UAE, you will need the official title for the vehicle or the original purchase invoice to prove that the car is yours. This is also called the Vehicle Ownership Certificate. Generally, you are not permitted to ship a car outside the country if it is under lien.

You will also need to know the approximate value of the vehicle as this is needed to determine the cost of the duties and taxes to be applied, which are usually 5% of the invoice value.

The costs to ship your vehicle to the UAE will vary depending on your country and port of export and, of course, the shipping company you use. Shipping companies usually charge a flat rate for this service. The price increases if you hire a clearing agent to assist you with clearing customs once the car arrives. I elected to do this myself.

I shipped a 9-year old Sports Utility Vehicle valued at $7,000 from the United States using a port in Florida to the Jebel Ali port in Dubai. I paid $1,800 for this service. From there, the car was transported to Abu Dhabi using a recovery vehicle because you are not allowed to drive an unregistered car on the roads.

Here is the breakdown of the total costs that I paid to clear customs once the car arrived in Dubai.

S. No	Description	Amount (Dhs)
1	Custom Duty	1,266.00
2	Import Registration	120.00
3	Duty Port Authority (DPA)	345.00
4	Clearing Charges	250.00
5	Vehicle Inspection	350.00
6	Recovery Vehicle Transport	400.00
7	Gate Pass	90.00
8	Car Battery Charge	60.00
9	Service Charge	200
10	VCC	150.00
	Total	3,231.00

There are several clearing agents available in Dubai to assist you with clearing customs if you elect not to hire a company to handle to entire process for you. Be prepared to negotiate the price for each of the fees charged with the exception of the duty and taxes. The fees are not set. If you do not negotiate, do not be surprised if you are quoted a price that contains a 100% markup for some fees. I shared the price I paid with you to give you a ballpark of what you should expect to pay. If you are not the type of person that likes to haggle to get the best price, you may want to enlist the services of a clearing agent on the front-end to handle everything for you.

GETTING A DRIVER'S LICENSE

Driving in the UAE requires a driver's license. A UAE driver's license allows you to drive freely in any of the seven emirates. You are allowed to drive temporarily using a valid, unexpired driver's license obtained from home or using an International Driving License. However, once you have obtained your Emirates Id (residence Id) you will need to get a UAE license in order to drive legally. Converting your driver's license to a UAE license is easy and can be done in an afternoon. It is important to note, however, that only licenses from the following countries can be directly converted without going to driving school and taking a road test:

Australia, Austria, Bahrain, Belgium, Canada, Denmark, Finland, France, Germany, Greece, Hong Kong, Ireland, Italy, Japan, South Korea, Kuwait, Luxemburg, Netherlands, New Zealand, Norway, Oman, Poland, Portugal, Qatar, Romania, Saudi Arabia, Serbia, Singapore, Slovakia, South Africa, Spain, Sweden, Switzerland, Turkey, the United Kingdom and the United States of America

It has been said that acquiring a driver's license is easier in Abu Dhabi and cheaper. For one, the Traffic and Licensing Department in Abu Dhabi has longer working hours than the Dubai Traffic Department. Here are step-by-step instructions on how to obtain a driver's license in Abu Dhabi and Dubai.

How to Get a Driver's License in Abu Dhabi

Before you head to the Traffic and Licensing Department you will need to have your current driver's license translated into Arabic. Like any service, the cost can vary depending on where you go. Expect to pay about 50 Dhs to have your license translated. Here are the next steps you will need to take to obtain your license in Abu Dhabi:

1. Gather all your documents. You will need your passport, visa page, Emirates Id, current driver's license, and the translation.
2. Have an eye test completed. In Abu Dhabi, the eye test can be completed at the Traffic and Licensing Department. The cost is 15 Dhs.
3. At the Licensing Department, take a number from the customer service counter and wait. There is a separate line for women that is quicker, but the general wait should not take more than an hour.
4. When your number is called, go to the correct desk and give your previous license, translation, passport, and Emirates Id to the person serving you. After you pay 200 Dhs, the attendant will take your picture and hand you a new driver's license in about ten minutes.

If you do not have a license from your home country or your license is not from one of the approved countries, you will need to take driving lessons and a test. Here are the steps you will need to take:

1. Open a file with Emirates Driving Company (EDC); this will allow you to register for a driving theory

course. You will need to bring your passport, Emirates Id, two passport size pictures and your visa page with photocopies. The EDC is the only driving school in Abu Dhabi and it is located in Musaffah, the Industrial Area where car repairs are completed. The cost of the theoretical course is 830 Dhs.
2. When you have completed the required eight theory classes, you will need to pass the written test. The test cost 50 Dhs.
3. If you have never obtained a driver's license at all, you must also take a practical driving course of five lessons. The costs, depending on the intensity of the course you choose, ranges from 650 Dhs to 2,250 Dhs. If you fail any one of the five lessons, you will have to start from the beginning and repay for the classes.
4. To take the practical driving test, you will need to make an appointment with the Traffic and Licensing Department, which is located behind Mushrif Mall. Bring your passport, Emirates Id, and proof of passing the theory test. The costs to schedule a practical driving test is 50 Dhs.
5. Once you have passed the test, you can go to the Traffic and Licensing Department with a certificate of having passed the test and complete steps 1 - 4 above in the preceding section.

How to Get a Driver's License in Dubai

Getting a driver's license in Dubai is very similar to the process in Abu Dhabi. If you have never driven before or you do not have a driver's license from one of the approved countries you must undergo training.

Here are the steps:

1. Register for a driving license course in one of the authorized driving schools by opening an RTA file. Bring your passport with residence stamp and Emirates Id.
2. Get an eye test completed and bring the receipt to the driving school.
3. Take a driving theory test that consists of 8 hours of lecture before starting practical training classes. The costs to take the test is 200 Dhs. The theory test can be taken at five authorized driving schools:
    i. Al Ahli Driving School (10 branches)
    ii. Belhasa Driving School (18 branches)
    iii. Dubai Driving Center (13 branches)
    iv. Emirates Driving Institute (53 branches/mall counters)
    v. Galadari Driving School (14 branches)
4. There is a pre-evaluation test for students who have signed up for classes to evaluate their driving experience.
5. After passing the theory test and pre-evaluation test (if required), students can begin their practical training.
    i. Students who do not possess a driving license (from any country) have to register for 40 classes.
    ii. Students possessing a driving license that is 2 - 5 years old from their home country have to take 30 classes.

    iii. Students possessing their country's license that is more than 5 years old have to take 20 classes.
6. After completing the practical training classes, your instructor will advise you to book your RTA parking test and assessment test.
7. After clearing your assessment test, you will complete your highway training before going to the final road test.
8. Take the road test. On the date assigned, go with your passport, Emirates Id, driving file, and two photos to the RTA License Section as advised by your driving school. Complete the application form and pay 200 Dhs for the road test. When your name is called, go along with your RTA inspector to the designated car. You will be given a few minutes to demonstrate your driving skills.

Note: If you fail, you will have to register with your driving school for at least seven additional classes and get a new road test date. You will have to pay for the classes and road test again.

9. If you pass the road test, collect your approval form from your inspector and go to the Pass Counter. Submit your ID and pay 100 Dhs. Collect your test file and submit to the Control Counter. After processing, pay the required fee. In a few minutes, you will receive your driver's license.

If you have a valid driver's license from one of the 36 approved countries the process is much simpler.

Here are the steps:

1. Get an eye test completed. Give them two passport-sized photos and mention that it is for a driving license.
2. Go to the Dubai Traffic Department Driving License section in Al Ghusais from 7:30 AM to 2:30 PM on a working day. Ladies can go to the Ladies section, where the process will take less time. Remember to bring your Emirate Id, Passport with visa stamp, and original driver's license.
3. Complete the application form and submit all required documents to the officer.
4. Take signed documents from the officer and pay 360 Dhs to the cashier.
5. Submit all documents at the Data Entry Counter.
6. Your name will be called and you will have your picture taken.
7. After a few minutes, you will receive your license.

THE HIDDEN COST OF DRIVING
Traffic Tickets

There is a hidden cost of driving in the UAE – traffic tickets. If you plan to drive frequently and travel between the emirates, at some point you will receive a traffic violation. There are speed cameras lining the streets and highways in every direction that will take a picture of your car if you are traveling 20 kilometers over the speed limit. A speeding ticket will costs you 600 Dhs, or $163.

The license plate will allow the vehicle to be traced back to the registered owner. The owner will be notified with a text message stating the time and date of the infraction. If you are driving a rental car, the rental company will be notified and you will be asked to pay the charge at the end of the billing period.

If you are observant, you may notice police officers stationed on bridges observing cars passing along the highway underneath them. They are taking pictures of speeders and drivers changing lanes without indicating. Not using your turning signal can get you 400 Dh ticket.

Dubai police are more sophisticated. Instead of parking on bridges, they drive around in unmarked cars taking pictures of traffic violators. You may not notice they were monitoring you until you get a text message on your phone alerting you of a traffic violation.

Driving Fees

Drivers traveling through Dubai have to pay for Salik. Salik, meaning open or clear, is Dubai's road toll system that operates without tollbooths or barriers. Unless you drive a rental car, you will be personally responsible for purchasing a Salik sticker tag and affixing it to your windshield. The sticker is linked to your prepaid Salik account. You can purchase a Salik tag online via the RTA website or at a gas station. All you need to do is install the tag and make sure your prepaid account has enough money in it to cover your Salik charges. Luckily, just about every mall has a kiosks station where you can recharge your prepaid account. Many banks also have an online feature that allows you to recharge your account.

Each time you drive through a Salik toll gate, the Salik sticker on your windshield is electronically detected and scanned by radio frequency identification (RFID) technology and 4 Dhs is automatically debited against your prepaid Salik account. You do not need to stop or even slow down when you pass through a Salik toll gate. Salik is a cleverly designed, free flowing system that works automatically.

Drivers can avoid paying Salik fees by using alternatives routes but this will be difficult and dramatically increase your commute time.

Presently, there are six toll gates:

- Al Safa (Sheikh Zayed Road)
- Al Barsha (Sheikh Zayed Road)
- Al Garhoud Bridge (Sheikh Zayed Road)
- Al Maktoum Bridge (Umm Hurair Road)
- Al Mamzar (Al Ittihad Road)
- Airport Tunnel (Beirut Street)

Parking Fees

Most street parking in Abu Dhabi, Dubai, and Sharjah is governed by parking meters. After feeding coins into the machine, you get a ticket to display on your dashboard. Parking monitors actively patrol public parking areas throughout the day searching for parking violators.

Abu Dhabi

Paid parking is administered by Mawaqif. Parking fees are applicable from 8:00 AM to 12:00 AM Saturday through Thursday. The minimum fee fare is 2 Dhs for one hour. The parking price goes up from there. You will pay 4 Dhs for two hours, 6 Dhs for 3 hours, up to 15 Dhs per day. Failing to pay or having an expired ticket can cost you 150 Dhs, if not more. Parking is free on Friday and public holidays and for people with special needs.

Mawaqif Payment Methods

Prepaid Cards for paid parking areas

Payments at the parking meters can be made by not only using coins but also by prepaid cards. Drivers can choose between cards for 50 Dhs and cards for 100 Dhs. They are available at Mawaqif Customer Service Centers.

Mobile Payment

The Mawaqif mobile service, called m-Mawaqif, allows drivers to pay parking fees using their mobile phone. After registering your Etisalat or Du mobile number online, you can top-up your account with a secure online credit card payment. You can use these funds on your account by sending an SMS in a pre-defined format to the number 3009. You will receive your permit via SMS. m-Mawaqif also sends a reminder message 10 minutes before the expiry of the permit. You can extend your permit for another hour by simply sending 'E' via SMS to the number 3009.

Residential Permits

Residential permits allow drivers to park in the paid parking areas that are located within the same sector they live in without paying the hourly or daily rates. Each household is allotted two residential permits, which are sector and vehicle specific. The annual fee is 800 Dhs for the first vehicle and 1,200 Dhs for the second vehicle. Residents can obtain residential permits from the Mawaqif Customer Service Centers.

Mawaqif Customer Service Centers

Several Customer Service Centers provide all necessary information on Mawaqif parking services. At these Centers, customers can buy prepaid parking cards and apply for residential permits.

The payment of parking violation tickets must be made at Mawaqif Customer Service Centers. Drivers who pay within 15 days of the violation will get a 25% discount on the total fine amount.

Alternatively, customers can call Mawaqif Call Centers 24 hours a day and 7 days a week by dialing 800 3009.

Customer Service Centers are located at:

- Main Bus Stations
- DMAT Main Branch – Al Maqta
- ADM Sheikh – Zayed Road
- ADM – AL Bateen Center
- ADM – Marina Mall

- Abu Dhabi Chamber of Commerce

Dubai

Paid parking is administered by RTA. Parking fees are applicable from 8:00 AM to 12:00 AM Saturday through Thursday. The parking fees start at 2 Dhs for one hour and go up from there depending on the parking zone. Parking is free from 1 PM to 4 PM and 9 PM to 8 AM daily, and on Friday and public holidays. Parking is free for people with special needs.

RTA Payment Methods

Mobile Payment

To pay for parking in Dubai, a motorist can either plug the meter with coins or use RTA's mparking service (mParking). This service allows you to pay for a virtual parking permit by using your Etisalat or Du mobile phone (the parking fee is added to your monthly bill) by simply sending an SMS text in a predefined format to 7275 (PARK) thus eliminating the need to walk to the Payment Display (P/D) machines and searching for coins. The mparking service will alert you via an SMS text prior to virtual permit expiry giving you the option to extend your parking period.

Only Dubai private registered cars can use this service without registering. To register, visit the RTA website to create a customer profile.

Prepaid Cards

A pre-paid card is available at supermarkets and grocery stores in denominations of 30 Dhs and 100 Dhs. The ticket amount is deducted from the balance on the card when inserted into the P/D machine.

Seasonal Parking Cards

These cards are available in different values and periods of validity. They are available in three-month, six-month, and annual validity. The seasonal card rates for roadside parking are 1,400 Dhs for three months, 2,500 Dhs for six months, and 4,500 Dhs for one year. The seasonal rates for parking lots are 700 Dhs for three months, 1,300 Dhs for six months, and 2,500 Dhs for one year. You simply display the parking card on your windshield to avoid a parking violation.

Nol Card

Nol Card is a smart card that enables you to pay for the use of various RTA transport modes in Dubai with a single card. You can use your Nol Card to travel on Dubai's Metro, Buses, Water Buses, Dubai Tram as well as pay for RTA's paid parking. Use your Nol Card to buy your parking ticket and the amount will be deducted from the card balance.

Smart Parking App

This is a free app for parking. This app was developed to help motorist in Dubai with the SMS parking provided by

RTA Dubai. To use the app, you must have a valid car plate registered in Dubai, a working mobile number (Etisalat or Du) with sufficient balance, permission to send SMS, and a GPS enabled smartphone to locate a parking zone.

CHAPTER 5

THE EMIRATI CULTURE

Knowing the culture is critical for developing friendships and good business relationships in the UAE. When it comes to mixing with locals, good cultural awareness and knowing the proper UAE etiquette will help you make the best first impression possible.

THE PEOPLE

UAE nationals are a proud people whose culture reflects Islam and the Bedouin, Arab culture, and this is depicted in their clothing, architecture, music, cuisine, and lifestyle. Islam is embedded in their way of life. Local people are supposed to pray five times a day so you will frequently see mosques scattered throughout the city and prayer rooms in public buildings like malls.

CULTURAL PRACTICES

Emirati men prefer to dress in a white garment called a kandora, which is similar to a long, ankle-length shirt made from cotton or wool, along with a head covering called a ghutra. During the winter months, you will typically see more variety in colors such as blue, black, brown, and gray. Western-style clothing is also getting popular now, especially among the younger generation.

Emirati women wear something similar to the men's kandora called an abaya, but they typically come in different styles. The abaya is typically a black over-garment that covers most parts of a woman's body. Some women wear western-styled clothing underneath the abaya, but they generally avoid wearing short, fitted clothing. Also, some women prefer to cover their faces in public. They also like wearing high heel shoes, the higher the heel the better.

CUISINE

Emirati food is a blend of many Middle Eastern and Asian cuisines due to the large influx of migrants that live and work in the region. Traditionally, due to the harsh desert conditions, the Emirati diet consisted mainly of meat, grain, and dairy. Meats consist of chicken and lamb. Lamb and mutton are the more favored meats, then goat and beef. Camels are highly prized for their milk, and eating camel is normally reserved for special occasions. Seafood has also been part of the Emirati diet for centuries.

Muslims are prohibited from eating pork, so you will not find it on any Arab menus. Hotels and restaurants typically have pork substitutes such as beef or chicken sausages and lunch meat. Luckily, for some, there are several grocery stores in the UAE, except in the Emirate of Sharjah, that sell pork meat in special sections inside the store. A few stores that sell pork include Choithrams, Spinney's, Waitrose Supermarket, Philippine Supermarket, West Zone Market Supermarket, and Al Maya Supermarket.

Despite being a Muslim country, the UAE has tried to make certain accommodations for non-Muslim residents. In return, and as a courtesy, consumers should be responsible and careful when carrying pork items during picnics or avoid displaying them in public. Even though the UAE is a very tolerant country, it is just good manners to be respectful of the local culture and religion.

THE DO'S AND DON'TS

UAE nationals are very hospitable so do not be surprised if you are invited to an Emirati's house for lunch or dinner or maybe a trip to their farm. You should know the proper etiquette when visiting an Emirati home.

1. You should either accept or decline the invitation. If you must decline, you should give a specific reason as to why you cannot attend. If you fail to do so or your reply is vague, the host may think you are not interested in having a relationship with them.
2. If you arrive at an Emirati house and women are with you, the women are expected to sit inside the house with other women. In the Emirati culture, women do not sit together with strange men.
3. At the entrance of the home, you may see a rack of shoes or a bunch of shoes aligned on the floor. This is an indication that you should remove your shoes. The host may give you a pair of slippers or socks to walk in.

If you do not want to get in trouble with the authorities and end up in jail or deported there are certain things you should not do. Provided are just a few things that you should adhere to while you are in the UAE.

Dress Code

Residents and visitors are expected to dress modestly, particularly in public places. Remember, the UAE is an Islamic country and the dress code is conservative. Although non-Muslim women are not expected to wear a traditional black abayah (a robe-like dress) and cover their head with a shayla (head gear worn by women) and men are not expected to wear a kandora (a long ankle length shirt-like covering made of cotton or wool), women should not wear clothing that exposes cleavage and short dresses and men should avoid wearing shorts that rise above the knee and tank tops in public. Swimwear is acceptable at private and public beaches or around swimming pools, but you should be covered up when you step away from these areas. Cross-dressing is not allowed and can get you in trouble with the police. Public nudity of any kind is an absolute no-no and will get you into serious trouble.

Drugs

I should not have to say this, but do not try to bring drugs into the UAE. You can bring medication with you if you have an attested prescription from a doctor, but if it can be mistaken for drugs, be careful.

Public Intoxication

Being drunk and disorderly in public is totally unacceptable, and may result in a fine or worse. Driving under the influence of alcohol is met with zero tolerance. If there is any doubt about whether you have had too much to drink, get a taxi. They are relatively cheap and there are plenty available.

<u>Eating During Ramadan</u>

Ramadan is the holy month in which Muslims commemorate the revelation of the Holy Quran. It is a time of fasting and Muslims abstain from all food and drink between dusk and dawn. At sunset, the fast is broken with the Iftar feast. Also during Ramadan, no live music or dancing is allowed.

During the Holy month of Ramadan, shops and restaurants often change their hours by closing during the day, and re-open an hour or two after sunset, and stay open later into the night. Food outlets and restaurants generally remain closed. Some may blackout their windows or offer takeaway services during the day for non-Muslims, and then open for Iftar after sunset.

Non-Muslims are required to respectfully refrain from eating, drinking or smoking in public places during daylight hours. Failure to comply could upset people that are fasting and lead to an official complaint and possible jail time.

<u>Photography</u>

It may seem like a small thing, but be careful when you take pictures in public places. Before snapping a picture of a national or resident of the UAE, especially if the subject is a woman, make sure you get their permission first. The same goes for taking video with your smartphone. If you fail to do this and your action is observed, your infraction can land you in jail. A Texas man on vacation with his son in Thailand was arrested while transiting at the Abu Dhabi International Airport for filming security guards that were inspecting his bags. The 59-year old man was detained, fined 10,000 Dhs ($2,722), and deported.

Showing Disrespect

You are expected to act and behave in a civil manner at all times. Noise disruptions, cursing, making obscene gestures and showing disrespect to others in public is forbidden. Also, never make the mistake of offending a national by disrespecting the country's leaders or any of the ruling families, as this will get you in trouble with the authorities.

Public Displays of Affection

Do yourself a favor and avoid kissing in public. Otherwise, you can attract unwanted attention. This includes nightclubs, hotels, beaches, and cars. You can hug or kiss children or other people when greeting them; however, you cannot kiss your spouse or significant other in a sexual way.

Social Media

Be cautious when using social media. Refrain from posting anything negative about the ruling families, or local religious and cultural traditions. While most things go unnoticed as they do in most parts of the world, there have been cases where postings on Facebook has gotten people in trouble. Remember, the UAE has state of the art surveillance technology. It never hurts to take precautions.

Chapter 6

Things To Do In The UAE

All work and no play makes Jack a dull boy. Luckily, the UAE has plenty of attractions to keep you from becoming dull. Depending on which emirate you live in, the only limitation to the number of extracurricular activities available is the amount of free time you have, how much you want to sleep, and how much discretionary income you have available for entertainment.

UAE ATTRACTIONS

Entertainment preferences are highly subjective and depend on your personality and current situation – whether you are an introvert or extrovert, thrill seeker or conservative, married or single, with or without children, you have a high-paying job or a low-paying job, etc. Fortunately, the UAE has something for everyone that matches personal preferences and budgets.

DUBAI

When it comes to entertainment and extracurricular activity, Dubai is the clear winner and the crowd favorite. Due to this fact, it is much harder to save money in Dubai because there are so many things to do, places to go, people to see, and ways to spend money. Here are just a few of the many indoor and outdoor attractions and activities Dubai has to offer.

Beaches

Jumeirah Beach Park is a wonderfully landscaped strip of beach on Jumeira Beach Road near the Jumeira Beach Hotel conveniently surrounded by cafes, fine restaurants, and shopping. Even on a hot day, there is plenty of shade available under one of the many umbrellas for rent. When you are not enjoying lying under the sun, you can BBQ in one of the designated areas or swim in the Arabian Gulf. Jumeirah Beach is a well known tourist attraction and the right place to show off your new bikini or six pack abs.

Al Mamzar Beach Park is based on the same design as Jumeirah Beach and is located at the other end of Dubai right along the border with the emirate of Sharjah.

Ski Dubai

After a day at the beach, you can trade in your bathing suit for a pair of skis and brave the slopes at Mall of the Emirates. The ski slopes are fashioned like a mountain resort and the cool temperature definitely makes the experience real. The cold air can be a welcome relief during the summer months when the temperature soars. Whether you want to ski, snowboard, or play on a toboggan, when you buy your ticket you are supplied with all the equipment you need. Who would have imagined you could go skiing in the desert.

The Burj Khalifa

Ride to the top in an express elevator and look down on Dubai from what is currently the tallest building in the world. Ticket prices start at 135 Dhs for an adult (12 years +) and 100 Dhs for a child (4 – 12 years) during non-prime hours. After you are done, take a nice stroll in the Burj Khalifa Park to experience the six water features, the palm tree lined walkways, gardens and flowering trees. The park area includes two tennis courts, a wading pool, and a children's playground.

Dubai Mall

Walking distance from the Burj Khalifa is Dubai Mall, an absolute must see. The mall is the world's largest shopping mall in terms of total area, and the fifth largest in gross leasable area. The mall is part of the Burj Khalifa complex, featuring over 1,200 shops. One of the many features within the mall is the world's largest Gold Souk with more than 200 retailers, Oasis Fountain Waterfall, Waterfront Atrium, SEGA indoor theme park, a 22-screen Cineplex, which is the largest in Dubai, KidZania, gold and jewelry outlets, a supermarket, organic food mart, an Olympic-sized ice skating rink, Dubai Aquarium and underwater zoo, 120 restaurants and cafes, and a 250-room luxury hotel. If you have the energy, you could spend your entire day trying to conquer this mall.

Desert Driving

Desert driving, also called dune bashing, is a desert adventure available in Dubai. Just meet at one of the designated spots for pickup and the driver will take you to a remote area where you can launch off the top of large sand dunes in a seven seat 4x4 vehicle. Often included in the price of these excursions is camel riding, henna painting, shisha smoking, and a buffet dinner. There is often music and belly dancing as well.

Camel Races

The camel racing season begins in October and is usually over by the end of February. Camel racing is a more relaxed and dusty affair than the Dubai World Cup. Although camel racing is a traditional sport and pastime, it has changed in recent years with the introduction of electronic jockeys to replace the young boys who used to ride the camels. Admission is free and families are welcome.

Dubai Parks and Resorts

Opening in December 2016, Dubai Parks and Resorts is the Middle East's largest integrated leisure and theme park destination. Spread over 25 million square feet, it features more than 100 rides and attractions, and consist of three theme parks: Bollywood Parks Dubai, Legoland Dubai, and Motiongate Dubai, and one water park - Legoland Water Park. The park also features Riverland Dubai, a themed retail and dining destination, as well as the Polynesian-themed family resort Lapita Hotel Dubai.

Soon to come, Six Flags Dubai will be the fourth theme park added to Dubai Parks and Resort. It is expected that the park will open its doors in late 2019 with an additional 27 rides and attractions.

Ticket prices start at 95 Dhs if you are a GCC resident and is 175 Dhs for nonresidents. An annual pass to only one of the theme parks is 275 Dhs. An all parks annual pass is 525 Dhs.

Global Village

Everything is big in Dubai, and Global Village does not disappoint claiming to be the world's largest tourism, leisure, shopping, and entertainment project. Every year, Global Village draws and attracts over 5 million visitors. It is the region's first cultural, entertainment, family and shopping destination.

When you are not shopping at one of the sponsored country exhibits, you can enjoy one of the many stage shows, concerts, and cultural shows available at night each day.

Tickets can be purchased in advance online or you can pay at the gate. The price is 15 Dhs per person. Global Village opens in October and closes the end of March. It operates 7 days a week, and opens its gates to visitors from Saturday to Wednesday from 4 PM to 12:00 AM, and opens until 1:00 AM on Thursday, Friday, and public holidays. For the best deals, go in March when venders are desperate to get rid of inventory.

Night Life

Dubai has a fun and exciting nightlife that no country in the Middle East can match. In fact, Dubai has taken on somewhat of a Las Vegas reputation – what happens in Dubai stays in Dubai. As long as you keep it indoors and out of sight, and avoid public intoxication, no one seems to care. There is a party going on somewhere each night of the week at one of the seemingly endless number of hotels. There is also a weekly holiday called "Ladies Night" and the best thing about it is that it occurs literally every night. You can dance to the beat or sip an alcoholic beverage as the DJ pumps the latest dance, R&B, and hip-hop music from the stage.

If you are single and looking to mingle, even though the UAE is a Muslim country, because there are so many expats living here some people are able to casually date. Dating apps like Plenty of Fish, OKCupid, Match, etc., actually work.

Friday Brunch

Brunch is a famous Dubai institution that will never go out of style. The price of a good brunch can be quite high at times (300+ Dhs), but it also includes as much alcohol and food you can consume, so people do not seem to mind. Plus, many locations also accept coupons from Groupon and The Entertainer apps.

Brunches are divided into 8 categories:

- Foodie Brunches

- Party Brunches
- Parent Friendly Brunches
- Evening Brunches
- Outdoor Brunches
- Family Friendly Brunches
- Quirky Casual Brunches
- Brunch and Swim Packages

ABU DHABI

Abu Dhabi offers a more family friendly environment. While there are not as many things to do and the nightlife is not as vibrant, there are many attractions to keep you from getting bored. Here are just a few of the attractions and activities available.

<u>The Grand Mosque</u>

The Sheikh Zayed Grand Mosque is the largest mosque in the country. This majestic structure was constructed between 1996 and 2007 to serve as a key place for worship for Friday gathering and Eid prayers. It can accommodate 40,000 worshippers while the main prayer hall can hold over 7,000 visitors.

The mosque's features are impressive and an immaculate display of artistry, design, and precision. No expense was spared. It features 82 domes, over 1,000 columns, 24-karat gold gilded chandeliers, and the world's largest hand knotted carpet.

Abu Dhabi Corniche

The Corniche Road spreads across eight kilometers of manicured waterfront that includes children's play areas, separate cycle and pedestrian pathways, cafés and restaurants, and the Corniche Beach.

Some 30,000 to 50,000 visitors flock to the Corniche every month, enjoying three separate sections for families, singles, and the general public. There are more than 1,100 free parking spaces within a five-minute walk. The charge is 10 Dhs ($2.72) for entry into the family and singles section. Entry to the public beach is free.

Emirates Palace

Emirates Palace is a must-see five star luxury hotel consisting of 394 residences, including 92 suites and 22 residential suites. The majority of the suites are furnished in gold and marble. The main primary building houses an expansive marble floor and a large patterned dome outfitted in gold. The facilities include two spa facilities, over 40 meeting rooms, a 1.3-kilometer long beach, a marina, two helicopter landing pads, a ballroom that accommodates up to 2,500 people, various luxury shops, and international restaurants.

Ferrari World

If you love cars, then you should definitely visit the world's first Ferrari-branded theme park. The theme park is home to a winning mix of Ferrari inspired rides and attractions, the biggest Ferrari store, and a range of authentic Italian dining options, so there are plenty of choices for the whole family.

Beneath its iconic red roof it houses numerous high-adrenaline rides including the spectacular new Flying Aces ride, featuring the highest rollercoaster loop in the world, the world's fastest rollercoaster, Formula Rossa, with a top speed of 250 kilometers per hour in 4.9 seconds, family-friendly attractions, state-of-the-art simulators, electric-powered go-karts, live shows and an inspiring treasure of racing memorabilia.

Yas Waterworld

Yas Waterworld is a waterpark located on Yas Island in Abu Dhabi. The waterpark houses 40 rides, slides, and attractions. The park is home to the Bandit Bomber, which is the longest suspended roller coaster in the Middle East at over 550 meters long. The waterpark has a variety of attractions grouped into four categories: Adrenaline Rush, Exciting Adventures, Moving & Grooving and finally, Young Fu.

Warner Bros. World

Warner Bros. is an indoor amusement park in Abu Dhabi. The park features characters from the Warner Bros. franchise, such as Loney Tunes, DC Comics, Hana-Barbera, and others. The park is located on Yas Island near Ferrari World and Yas Waterpark.

The Louvre Abu Dhabi

The Louvre Abu Dhabi was established on November 8, 2017. If the name sounds familiar, that is because Abu Dhabi paid $525 million to use the name, with an additional $747 million to be paid in exchange for art loans, special exhibitions, and management advice. The museum is part of a 30-year agreement between Abu Dhabi and the French government. Inside you can find artwork from around the world.

AL AIN

Despite being smaller than Abu Dhabi and Dubai in terms of area and population, there are still quite a few things to do and places to visit. Here are just a few of them.

Al Ain Oasis

In the heart of the city, the Al Ain Oasis was opened as the UAE's first curated UNESCO World Heritage site visitor experience. Spread over 1,200 hectares (nearly 3,000 acres) and containing more than 147,000 date palms of up to 100 different varieties, this impressive oasis is filled with palm plantations, many of which are still working farms.

The cool, shady walkways transport you from the heat and noise of the city to a tranquil haven; all you will hear is birdsong and the rustle of the palm fronds. The site introduces visitors to the delicate oasis eco-system and the importance it has played in the development of the emirate. The oasis landscape of Al Ain is shaped by a complex shared water supply based on both wells and 'aflaj', the UAE's traditional irrigation system. Al Ain Oasis has plenty of working examples of the falaj which have been used for centuries to tap into underground wells.

Sheikh Zayed Palace Museum

Get a peek at how Sheikh Zayed lived before oil was discovered and the capital was relocated to Abu Dhabi. Located on the western edge of Al Ain Oasis, the Palace was the home of the late Sheikh Zayed bin Sultan Al Nahyan and was built in 1937. It was converted into a museum in 1998 and opened to the public in 2001. The original structure was comprised of a private residence for the ruler and his family within a complex of beautifully landscaped courtyards.

The 1998 renovation saw the addition of two new buildings, one of which houses the administration and displays gifts dedicated to the museum from the local community, while the other presents a family tree of the Al Nahyan family, offering visitors the opportunity to learn about the country's ruling family and lineage. The design of the new buildings adopts elements of local architecture, reflecting traditional design tastes, including towers added to the main entrance of the palace that is similar to Al Jahili Fort. The palace interior was renovated to reflect traditional designs, and the furniture is typical of the era it was built in.

Paying homage to the heritage of Sheikh Zayed, the tent that he used to host guests during the winter has been erected in the palace. The tent simulates the way of life Sheikh Zayed was proud of, and allows visitors to learn about the Bedouin heritage, history and renowned Arabic hospitality.

Admission to the museum is free.

<u>Jebel Hafeet</u>

Rising 1,240 meters, Jebel Hafeet is the emirate's highest peak, and the UAE's second. This lofty rocky height, which stands guard over Al Ain and borders Oman, is forged out of limestone that has been weathered over millions of years. Significant fossil discoveries have been made in the area, which are vital pieces in the jigsaw of the city's ancient history.

Over 500 ancient burial tombs dating back 5,000 years have been found in the Jebel Hafeet foothills.

You can drive or, if you have the stamina, cycle to the top via a winding highway, which is described as "among the world's greatest driving roads." Once you reach the top, you will be rewarded with spectacular views over Al Ain. After you are done, you can take a break at the Mercure Jebel Hafeet hotel near the Jebel's peak.

Chapter 7

Making Money In The UAE

With every passing year the UAE, particularly Dubai, is becoming a dream destination for professionals from all over the world to come work. People are attracted to the UAE because of the career growth opportunities, higher salaries, luxurious lifestyle, safety, and world-class infrastructure. In a 2016 survey, deVere Group, an independent financial advisory company, reported that Dubai is the second most popular destination for aspiring bankers in the world. New York still holds the top spot. Abu Dhabi claimed the fifth position on the list. With so much to offer, it is no wonder why so many people desire to live and work in the UAE.

HOW TO GET A JOB IN THE UAE

Finding a plane ticket and booking a hotel to come to the UAE is easy. How easy is it to find a job? With so many people clamoring to find a job in the UAE, this can be more difficult.

When it comes to finding a job, the UAE is no different from other countries; it helps if you know someone. Not every job opening is posted on a company's website or on public job listings. In fact, many companies use word of mouth or placement agencies to identify suitable candidates. It will help tremendously if you can find someone that will put your résumé/CV forward. Times have changed. It is not like 15 years ago when you could jump on a plane, come to the UAE, and find a job within 30 days before your visa expired.

The good news is that the job market in Dubai and Abu Dhabi is dynamic. Many people come to work for a few years and then leave. Therefore, positions are always coming available. To find an opening, you have to make sure that you are rightly positioned and can be easily identified when an opportunity becomes available.

I got my position after being contacted by a recruiter who saw my profile on LinkedIn. I know several people that acquired their position this way. If you have not already, I strongly encourage you to create an employment profile on a website highly frequented by recruiters.

Provided below are popular job sites where you can search for jobs, create an employment profile, and upload your résumé/CV.

- Bayt
- DubaiClassified.com
- Dubizzle
- Emirates Ads
- EmiratesVillage.com

- Expatriates.com
- Efinancialcareers-gulf.com
- LinkedIn

- Gulf News
- Jobs123.com
- Khaleej Times
- Kugli.com
- The Emirates Network
- TotalJobs
- AuthorityJob.com
- Zoozi

After creating an employment profile and uploading your résumé/CV to a highly viewed employment website, the next step is to develop a relationship with at least three recruiters from different recruitment agencies. They will let you know whether you have the requisite skills for the position you want and what you may need to do to improve your success.

Here is a list of the Top 10 recruitment agencies in Dubai.

Jivaro Partners

Jivaro Partners is a marketing and communication agency. Its focal points are advertising, PR, digital, events, and branding. It recruits talented people with experience in event planning and creative design, which includes the following:

- Creative Director
- Copywriter
- Planning Manager
- Account Executive
- Art Director
- Account Manager
- Graphics Designer
- Client Services Director

ESP International

ESP International is an international recruitment agency that provides expertise to its customers in the following fields:

- Engineering services
- Assembly services
- Furniture assembly
- Global supplier
- Vendor optimization
- Technology for better services

MCG & Associates

MCG & Associates is a recruitment agency in Dubai who recruits talent for the communication and deglitch sectors. The areas they recruit are as follows:

- PR Agency and communications
- Client servicing
- Creative designing
- Data, insight and analytics
- Information security and technology
- Media publishing
- Project management
- Sales and business development

Robert Murray and Associates

Robert Murray and Associates' goal is to transform organizations and in turn, touch the lives of the clients by adding substantial value to the international leadership and executive search industry.

- Plant General Manager
- Director – Polymer (Europeans)
- Vice President – Energy
- Infrastructure Manager
- Compensation & Benefits Manager
- Sr. Recruitment Consultant

Careerjet Dubai

Careerjet is a recruitment agency with a proven record of providing multi-dimensional jobs rendering to your skillset. They do not specialize in providing jobs in a particular market or specialization. Their long list of jobs ranges from Senior AX Business Analyst to Dance Teacher.

Hays Dubai

Hays Dubai recruits candidates from all over the world. It has offices in Abu Dhabi and Dubai and headhunts across the region in the following areas:

- Contingent recruitment
- Executive search
- Multiple hiring and recruitment
- Contracting

NADIA Recruitment Agency

NADIA Recruitment Agency is one of the oldest recruitment agencies in Dubai helping to find jobs for candidates. It has the ability to help job seekers match the relevant position with their qualifications and skillset. They provide the following services to clients:

- Banking and Finance
- Consumer Products
- Education
- Engineering
- Healthcare
- Information Technology and Service
- Manufacturing, Oil and Gas, Shipping
- Logistics sectors

BAC Middle East

BAC Middle East is the region's first recruitment agency in Dubai providing a job for every kind of candidate to companies across the region. Their list of jobs include:

- Engineering and technical jobs
- Management
- Marking, PR and communications

Charter House

Charter House is one of the largest recruitment agencies in Dubai. They recruit for the following areas:

- Accounting and finance
- Architecture and design
- Banking
- Construction
- Human Resource
- IT and telecom
- Supply chain
- Logistics

Michael Page

Michael Page provides career consulting to job seekers giving companies and clients an opportunity to recruit talented employees. They provide recruitment for:

- Advisory
- Engineering
- Information Technology
- Legal

- Manufacturing
- Health & Life Sciences
- Procurement & Supply Chain
- Real Estate & Construction

AVAILABLE WORK OPPORTUNITIES

You stand the best chance of finding a job where there is high demand. Engineers, accountants, and sales executives are among the top skills in high demand today in the UAE due to new real estate developments that seem to be popping up each day. There is also significant demand for customer and healthcare services staff, as well as information technology professionals. Teachers are also in high demand with many job opportunities to work for private and public schools. There are also plenty of opportunities for those that can work as a receptionist, administrator and office assistant, although these jobs will not pay a high salary.

One fact worth noting is the workweek begins on Sunday and ends on Thursday. Skilled professionals generally work five days a week whereas unskilled laborers have only one day off. The government sector has a five-day workweek. Jobs in the service industry typically adhere to a six-day workweek.

SALARIES AND WAGES

There is no minimum wage for expats in the UAE so be prepared to negotiate your salary. There is a very wide range in salary for most jobs. Do your research to find out what the salary range is for your qualifications. Otherwise, you could end up making far less than you are worth. Do not accept a low paying job believing that once you have proven yourself your pay will be adjusted accordingly. I have heard numerous cases where promises were made and not kept. Get the money you desire coming in the door.

Your salary and allowances will have a vital role in determining your standard of living and quality of life. The UAE is a great place to live if you have money, but it can be miserable if you do not. The good thing is that the income you earn is tax-free. That is right, tax-free. Not having to pay taxes on your salary can help you save a sizeable amount of money. Not only can this money be used to pump your savings account, it can be used to afford certain luxuries that would otherwise be unattainable.

Here is a list of the highest paying jobs and their salary and allowances.

1. Chief Marketing Officers
   Average monthly pay including allowances: 95,000 Dhs and Salary range is 80,000 Dhs to 90,000 Dhs

2. Accounting, Finance Professionals

Average monthly pay including allowances: 75,000 Dhs and Salary range is 55,000 Dhs to 90,000 Dhs

3. Lawyers
   Average monthly pay including allowances: 77,000 Dhs and Salary range is 60,000 Dhs to 106,000 Dhs

4. Doctors
   Average monthly pay including allowances: 73,460 Dhs

5. Bankers
   Average monthly pay including allowances: 70,000 Dhs and Salary range is 63,750 Dhs to 77,500 Dhs

6. Engineers
   Average monthly pay including allowances: 62,000 Dhs and Salary range is 40,000 Dhs to 68,000 Dhs

7. IT Managers
   Average monthly pay including allowances: 60,000 Dhs and Salary range is 50,000 Dhs to 80,000 Dhs

8. Merchandiser
   Average monthly pay including allowances: 55,000 Dhs and Salary range is 36,500 Dhs to 52,500 Dhs

9. Actuaries
   Average monthly pay including allowances: 55,000 Dhs and Salary range is 30,000 Dhs to 80,000 Dhs

10. Pilots
    Average monthly pay including allowances: 52,500 Dhs and Salary range is 30,000 Dhs to 75,000 Dhs

11. Restaurant General Managers
    Average monthly pay including allowances: 50,000 Dhs and Salary range is 25,000 Dhs to 70,000 Dhs

12. Creative Director
    Average monthly pay is 48,330 Dhs and Salary range is 35,000 Dhs to 68,000 Dhs

13. Public Relations Managing Director
    Average monthly pay is 85,000 Dhs to 100,000 Dhs

14. Supply Chain Manager/Executive
    Earn 75,000 Dhs monthly

15. Call Center Manager
    Earn 13,932 Dhs monthly

16. Teachers
    Private School Teaching salary ranges from 9,000 Dhs to 15,000 Dhs plus accommodation

17. Real Estate / Property Consultant
    Property consultant earns an average of 96,472 Dhs per year

Regardless of how much money you earn and whether you work in the private or public sector, you will be paid only once per month.

STARTING A BUSINESS

There are many people that come to the UAE to start a business, and many are rewarded handsomely for their risk taking. Indeed, the UAE has proven to be the land of opportunity for many entrepreneurs. For a long time now, Dubai has welcomed foreign capital and investment, and has worked hard to make it easy for entrepreneurs to do business. These efforts have not gone without notice. In the 2018 *Doing Business Report* published by the World Bank, the UAE ranked 21st, up five spots from 26th in 2017.

Unless your business operates in one of the free zones, you will need a UAE national as a partner, called a local 'sponsor', to control 51% of the business. In the majority of cases, the local sponsor is not involved in the day-to-day management of the business and only desires 10% – 15% of the net profit for their trouble. You should develop a good relationship with your sponsor so that they are ready to help you in sorting out any problems that can surface along the way with authorities.

Setting up your business in one of the Free Zones offers three important advantages:

- 100% ownership
- Fast startup
- Duty-free customs

If starting a business is your preference, there are some do's and don'ts that you will want to be mindful of.

Five Do's In Business Startup

1. Select a local sponsor, a UAE national for local business startup.
2. Select a Free Zone if you wish to own your business 100%.
3. Select a location that optimizes suitability, convenience, and costs.
4. Confirm your visa eligibility and requirement.
5. Hire a registration agent to take you through the process of business startup.

Five Don'ts in Business Startup

1. Do not register your company in a Free Zone without looking at available office sizes and preconditions.
2. Do not make firm plans based only on published information.
3. Do not choose a license category blindly without confirming if it follows your business model.
4. Do not open a bank account without confirming the bank charges.
5. Do not sign a sponsorship with a local sponsor without a written legal agreement.

FOREIGN INVESTORS

On May 22, 2018, the Cabinet announced a decision that will allow 100% ownership of UAE-based businesses for international investors. This is excellent news for foreign investors that want to operate a business in the UAE.

Specific details that will explain the requirements of how to qualify for 100% ownership is waiting to be released.

CHAPTER 8

EDUCATION IN THE UAE

Moving to the UAE will be an exciting, thrilling experience, and perhaps, even a bit scary. There will be many important decisions you will have to make. Some of them can be complex. The complexity increases if you have school-aged children. In addition to searching for accommodation, buying furniture, getting familiar with your new environment, obtaining a driver's license, setting up a bank account, etc., you also have to enroll your kids in school.

Finding a school that meets your expectations and your budget can get a little tricky, especially if you do not know anyone in the UAE with children or know who to ask for guidance. Favorably, this chapter can answer some of the questions that you may have and point you in the right direction.

THE SCHOOL SYSTEM

There is two types of schools available to send your children – public and private school. Both offer education programs for children at the kindergarten (US) and nursery (British) age level and advance to elementary (US) and primary (British), and on to secondary school where a child can obtain a high school diploma (US), International Baccalaureate (IB) diploma, or sit for the IGCSE and A level (British) tests.

Public schools are generally reserved for UAE nationals. I say "generally" because expats are allowed to send their children to a public school. You will be charged tuition, but the amount is much less than private schools. Classes are taught in Arabic by teachers that are usually from Egypt, Jordan, Syria, Palestine, and other Middle Eastern countries. This is where expats usually lose interest in investigating public school options further, and for good reason. Although classes taught in English have been introduced into schools in Abu Dhabi and a few select schools in the other emirates, unfortunately, the education received in many cases is marginal at best. Learning standards and expectations are not very high and discipline is generally lacking. Quite often, children are not encouraged to learn. Despite these very unfortunate deficiencies, children still manage to receive high grades due to an environment that encourages cheating, in many cases aided by the teacher themselves. However, all public schools are not poorly run with low academic standards, but the sad fact is that the majority of them still are. For this reason, many UAE nationals, who understand and value the importance of education, send their children to one of the many private schools.

Most expatriates send their children to a private school where the curriculum taught matches their home country. Fortunately, Abu Dhabi and Dubai have many schools to choose from where instruction follows the American, Australian, British, Canadian, French, Indian, Japanese, and International Baccalaureate curriculum.

You will have fewer options if you live in one of the other five emirates.

You will need to do your research to find the best school for your children. A good place to start is a website called whichshooladviser.com. This website will allow you to research schools by emirate, curriculum, and the rating it received in the most recent school inspection provided by ADEC (Abu Dhabi Education Council) or KHDA (Knowledge and Human Development Authority). ADEC is the education authority for Abu Dhabi and KHDA is the rating agency responsible for the growth and quality of private education in Dubai.

Apply to your school of choice as early as possible, as soon as the enrollment period begins. For the best schools, available seats fill up quickly and many of these schools have a waiting list. Applications are usually accepted via the school's website.

PAYING FOR SCHOOL

The annual fee to attend school spans a wide range from as low as 2,000 Dhs to over 100,000 Dhs. In 2017, the average annual fee in Abu Dhabi was 27,700 Dhs and 34,700 Dhs in Dubai. Some employers will provide a supplement to employees with children to help defray the cost of tuition. The employer determines the amount. Before you accept a work contract, be sure to find out how much the company will contribute towards tuition. Most companies will not pay for other school-related expenses such as school uniforms, bus services, food, academic tests, and after-school activities. This must be funded out of pocket.

Most reputable schools post the total costs of tuition and transportation fees on the school's website. The methods in which payment is received varies depending on the school. Most payments are made in cash, check, or by wire transfer. Tuition fees must be paid before the first day of school (termly or annually). For new students enrolling, a non-refundable registration fee totaling 5% of the annual tuition fees is charged if you accept a place at the school. This registration fee will be deducted from tuition fees when the student takes up their reserved seat. As with all private for-profit enterprises, the costs of their services and fees will vary. It will be incumbent upon you to identify a school that matches your budget. Fortunately, whichschooladvisor.com is available to help you with your search.

I advise you to pay tuition and bus fees before the beginning of each term, not the full amount owed for the year in advance. Paying the full annual amount in advance is not advised because trying to get a refund of any pre-paid amounts can be a difficult and timely process. If any of the money for tuition is provided by your employer, and you leave before completing your contract, you will be required to refund the unused portion. Any amount not refunded will be subtracted from your end-of-service benefit.

HOMESCHOOL

There are parents that chose to homeschool their children. The UAE does not legally mandate that expatriates send their children to public or private school. However, the UAE does not encourage homeschooling. As such, the UAE does not offer an accredited government endorsed homeschool curriculum. If you want to homeschool your children, you will have to search for an accredited homeschooling program endorsed by your home country and ensure that you keep proper documentation of your child's work and progression. Upon arriving, after asking around, it is common to find others homeschooling their children. Perhaps they would be willing to allow your children to participate in their homeschool program. Although this is not legal, many expats will make money on the side by offering education services to other parents who desire to homeschool their children.

COLLEGES & UNIVERSITIES

There are several colleges and universities in the UAE that offer a bachelors, masters, and doctoral degrees. These institutions include public and government run, and private universities and colleges. Some of the world's best universities have annex campuses in the UAE, mostly housed in Dubai Knowledge Village and Academic City.

Here is a list of some of the most popular universities in the UAE by Emirate.

Abu Dhabi Colleges and Universities

- Abu Dhabi University
- Khalifa University of Science, Technology and Research (KUSTAR)
- Abu Dhabi School of Management (ADSM)
- New York Film Academy, Abu Dhabi
- University of Strathclyde Business School, Abu Dhabi
- Rabdan Academy
- Syscoms College Abu Dhabi
- The Petroleum Institute
- New York University (NYU) Abu Dhabi
- Abu Dhabi University Knowledge Group (ADUKG)
- Abu Dhabi Men's College (ADMC)
- Abu Dhabi Women's College (ADWC)
- Al Hosn University
- Al Khawarizmi International College (KIC)
- Emirates College of Advanced Education (ECAE)
- Emirates Institute for Banking & Financial Studies (EIBFS)
- European International College (EIC)
- Fatima College of Health Sciences
- Institute of Applied Technology
- INSEAD Abu Dhabi

Al Ain Colleges and Universities

- Al Ain University of Science and Technology
- Al Jaheli Institute of Science and Technology

- UAE University, Al Ain
- Abu Dhabi University, Al Ain
- HCT Al Ain Men's College
- UAEU College of Business Economics

Dubai Colleges and Universities

- Hult International Business School
- S P Jain School of Global Management
- Murdoch University, Dubai
- Al Dar University College
- Birla Institute of Technology and Science, Pilani
- University of Dubai (UD)
- University of Wollongong in Dubai (UOWD)
- Rochester Institute of Technology (RIT Dubai)
- MODUL University Dubai
- American University in Dubai (AUD)
- Heriot Watt University Dubai Campus
- Canadian University of Dubai (CUD)
- SAE Institute
- Manipal University Dubai
- Emirates Aviation University
- Middlesex University Dubai
- Institute of Management Technology, Dubai
- Synergy University Dubai
- EMDI Institute of Media and Communication
- University of Strathclyde Business School UAE

Sharjah Colleges and Universities

- Westford School of Management, Sharjah
- Al Qasima University (AQU)

- American University of Sharjah (AUS)
- Skyline University College
- Sharjah Women's College (SWC)
- Etisalat University College
- University of Sharjah
- Khalifa University Sharjah
- Police Sciences Academy
- HCT – Sharjah Men's College
- Sharjah Institute of Technology

Ras al-Khaimah Colleges and Universities
- American University of Ras Al Khaimah (AURAK)
- Emirates Munnar Catering College, RAK
- RAK Medical and Health Sciences University
- Ittihad University

Ajman Colleges and Universities
- Ajman University
- Gulf Medical University
- Global Learning Center (GLC)

Umm Al Quwain Colleges and Universities
- Emirates Canadian University

Chapter 9

Shipping And Mail Service

As strange as this may sound, in spite of the UAE's amazing infrastructure and wealth, the county has yet to develop a full post system. Therefore, online shopping is not as popular as it is in other parts of the world.

MAIL DELIVERY

Mail delivery to your home does not work very well because homes do not really have addresses. If you are having a package or a special item delivered like your Emirates Id or debt card, you will likely have to direct the deliveryman to a nearby landmark or a well-known building. Many people have learned how to use the Whatsapp feature 'send location' to direct the delivery driver to their specific location. Otherwise, get used to providing good verbal directions.

To get around this problem, for most people in Dubai and other UAE locations, their primary address is their place of work, and it is quite common for people to receive mail at their work location.

It is actually quite logical when you think about it. Legally, your sponsor is liable for you and your actions while you are a resident in the UAE. If you do not have a sponsor, unless you own property, you will not have a residency visa. Therefore, it follows that the most reliable way to make contact with you is through your sponsor, usually your employer.

How does this work? If you work for a medium to large organization, it will most likely have a company Post Office Box at a local Emirates Post Office (see below). Someone within the company will be responsible for collecting the mail from this PO Box each week, or more often depending on the volume of mail received. The mail will be brought to the workplace, sorted, and either delivered to your desk or, more likely, placed in a personal post box or communal mail-receiving bin.

Amazingly, although this system sounds chaotic, it actually works quite well. I have not met anyone yet that should have received a letter or package this way and did not receive it. You can trust the work delivery address for your personal mail. For the majority of expatriates living in the UAE, this mail delivery system will meet most of their needs.

Here is an important point worth noting. There are no ZIP or Area Codes in the UAE. If you are asked to enter a ZIP Code as part of your address on an online order, just enter 000 in the box provided, but make sure the PO Box number is included as part of the actual physical address because that is where your mail will be sent.

EMIRATES POST

You can set up a post office box at an Emirates Post location nearest you to receive mail. Emirates Post, usually referred to as Empost, is the official postal operator for the UAE. There is a 70 Dh fee for new PO Box registration and the annual fee for this service is 250 Dhs.

I know several people that acquired a post office box to receive letters and packages but they all canceled it because they continued to receive mail intended for the previous owners.

If the PO Box option at one of the branches does not work for you, Emirates Post has added a whole range of mail delivery options.

<u>Villas</u>

This service entitles the customer to receive/send drop letters (all mail items, except registered mail, parcels and items that are subject to customs duty) through a private post box installed in front of the residence. This service is exclusively available for villa type houses only in selected areas. The annual cost of this service is 750 Dhs to receive/send mail one time each week.

<u>Residential Buildings</u>

If you live inside a residential building, you can have a PO Box installed to receive mail. There is a 70 Dh fee for new PO Box registration and the annual fee for this service is 450 Dhs.

<u>PO Box Mail Shelters</u>

Individuals living in residential and commercial areas can receive mail through PO Box shelters. There is a 70 Dh fee for new PO Box registration and the annual fee for this service is 300 Dhs.

METHODS TO BRING ITEMS INTO THE UAE

There are couriers that provide parcel and express mail services if you need to ship an item into/outside the country. The most notable ones are DHL Express and Federal Express.

Chapter 10

Leaving The UAE

Unless you marry an Emirati, every expat has an exit date. There is an appointed time when your employment contract will end and your resident status will expire. When this occurs, you will have only 30 days to get your affairs in order before you will have to leave the country. You want to avoid having to leave in a hurried manner and becoming like one of the many unfortunate examples you hear about when an expatriate has to leave prematurely or unexpectedly - they are unable to sell their furniture and end up leaving their car at the airport.

You did months of planning before relocating to the UAE. Similarly, leaving the UAE cannot be an overnight decision; it must be well planned and thought out. This chapter will discuss the things you should do to ensure that your exit is as smooth as possible.

CREATE AN EXIT FUND

I cannot stress this enough, plan for your departure by creating and maintaining an exit fund. Put a little money away each money so you will not have to use credit to finance your departure. If one of the reasons you came to the UAE was to work so that you can pay off debt, you should not create an additional debt for yourself when you leave.

An adequately funded exit fund will also provide you with more options when you evaluate how much you will be able to take with you when you leave. It goes without saying, the more savings you have the better. However, the size of your exit fund really depends on what you plan to take with you and what you have waiting for you in the place you plan to relocate. If you plan to return home, you may not need to take anything with you. But, if you will be going to another country to work or retire, instead of leaving with only the clothes on your back and whatever luggage you can carry, you can send your items with you in a shipping container. This way you will not have to purchase new items to replace the things you left behind.

SORTING OUT YOUR WORK CONTRACT

Notify your employer well in advance if you are quitting before your contract ends. You might be required to complete the notice period or forfeit pay or some of your end of employment benefit in lieu of it. Get your final payout and the money you are owed sorted with your employer. It is best for you to do this face-to-face instead of over the phone. For any disputes, contact the Ministry of Labor instead of your embassy. Hand over your passport to your employer to cancel your residence visa. Do not do this last minute as it could delay your departure or the immigration system could flag your name on a list. Once your visa is canceled, your medical insurance will be canceled as well. Be sure to return your medical insurance cards to your employer.

SORTING OUT BANK FORMALITIES

Before attempting to close your bank account, you need to make sure you have paid all outstanding bills, payments, loans, credit cards, and post-dated checks. If there are no liabilities, the account can be closed on the spot. However, if you received a credit card from one of the local banks in the UAE, closing your current or savings account and withdrawing the remainder of your money will not be as easy if the credit card account remains open. Even if your balance is zero, as long as your account remains open and you have the ability to access credit, the banks can, and often do, freeze your current account and deny you access to whatever cash you hold up to the credit limit on your credit card. If you have the luxury of knowing when you will be leaving in advance, payoff your credit card as early as possible and have the account closed.

Also, be aware that you cannot just empty your bank account and leave as your account can incur a monthly maintenance fee if your balance is zero or falls below a minimum balance. If your account goes into collections via the judicial system, you might get an unpleasant surprise the next time you visit the country or pass through any of the other GCC countries. It is better to have the account closed before you leave.

SORTING OUT YOUR ACCOMMODATION

If you stay in a leased or rented property, be sure to give the required notice period mentioned in your contract to the landlord. Leaving your accommodation without informing your landlord can incur you a large expense. There have been numerous cases where the contract has auto renewed without the tenant's knowledge and they were held liable for non-payment. If you leave without paying and a lawsuit is filed against you, your identity will be flagged and you will be arrested upon arrival the next time you enter the country. If you need an extension of a month or more, you need to renew your contract for the stipulated period accordingly. In cases where you end your contract and are moving out, return the keys to the landlord and collect any outstanding deposits you might be entitled to. Be sure to leave your accommodation in satisfactory condition or you may not receive the full amount of your deposit.

SORTING OUT THINGS WITH SERVICE PROVIDERS

Before leaving, cancel your contracts with your mobile phone provider, internet and telephone providers (Du or Etisalat). If you live in an accommodation and are responsible for the utilities, in the last few days before your departure, inform the power company to cancel your electricity and water connection. An un-canceled account can incur ongoing monthly expenses that you will be liable to pay. Be sure to keep your original receipts.

SELLING YOUR BELONGINGS

If you have items too large to take with you (furniture, cars, etc.) try posting them online at least a few weeks before you leave. Be sure to post good pictures and provide a good description of the item(s) for sale. You can post your items on websites like dubizzle.com and buzzon.khaleejtimes.com. If you plan ahead, you can sell your items and recoup some cash.

If you are in a hurry to leave, selling your car at a good price can be a bit more difficult. Still, it is best to post your car for sale online. The offer you get will be much better than approaching a car dealer to buy your car or visiting the nearest sellanycar.com or buyanycar.com locations. These companies will generally offer to purchase your car at prices that are laughable. I once took my 2004 Jaguar XJ6 to sellanycar.com to see what they would offer. The car was in good condition, no warning lights, fully loaded and polished, and new tires. I checked the model and year of manufacture on dubizzle and saw that the average price others were listing the same car for was around 15,000 Dhs. Sellanycar.com offered 1,500 Dhs, 90% below what I could reasonably expect to receive! I think you get my point.

SORTING OUT MATTERS WITH PETS

If you are bringing a pet to the UAE then you are probably familiar with the process and the related costs. Unfortunately, there are still too many people who acquire pets such as a dog or cat while they are here and are unaware of how much it costs to transport a beloved pet to another country. They are shocked when they find out how much it entails. Many people end up leaving their pet(s) behind with a friend or someone willing to take them in. Even worse, others have irresponsibly left their pets behind to fend for themselves. This is why Abu Dhabi and Dubai are overrun with cats.

As with most things nowadays, moving pets is not a cheap process and there are many factors to consider such as health certificates, fit to fly checks, airline charges, and veterinary fees. The costs can add up quickly and easily exceed 3,500 Dhs, depending on where you go for service and the location your pet will be transported to. Most people opt to use a pet transport service to save time and to make sure that things go smoothly; they do not have time to do the paperwork themselves. Additionally, these companies are familiar with the documents that are needed. If you decide to use a pet transport service, be sure to scrutinize every expense. Some of these relocation services will handle the whole process for you but will charge a staggering amount. Do your homework.

About the Author

Peyton Rogers is from Denver, Colorado. He attended Arizona State University and pursued a career in computer programming. Peyton moved to Abu Dhabi in 2015. In his spare time, Peyton enjoys cycling, scuba diving, traveling, and spending time with family and friends.

One Last Thing

If you enjoyed this book or found it useful, I would be grateful if you would post a positive review on Amazon. Your support really does make a difference and inspires others to take action.

Thank you again for your support.

Printed in Great Britain
by Amazon